DOCTORS OF PHILOSOPHY

Also by Muriel Spark

Muriel Spark

DOCTORS
OF
PHILOSOPHY

A Play

NEW YORK: ALFRED A. KNOPF
1966

First performance at
The New Arts Theatre Club, London
Tuesday, October 2nd, 1962

Presented by Michael Codron

CHARACTERS IN ORDER OF THEIR APPEARANCE:

Charlie Delfont	LAURENCE HARDY
Catherine, *his wife*	GWEN CHERRELL
Leonora, *Catherine's cousin*	URSULA HOWELLS
Mrs. S., *the daily help*	HAZEL HUGHES
Daphne, *the Delfonts' daughter*	KATHLEEN BRECK
Charlie Brown, *a lorry driver*	TOM BOWMAN
Young Charlie, *Daphne's boy friend*	TIM PREECE
Annie Wood, *Catherine's other cousin*	FENELLA FIELDING
Mrs. Weston, *Young Charlie's mother*	ANNE WOODWARD

The action takes place in Charlie Delfont's house overlooking the Regent's Canal. The play is in Three Acts. The lights are lowered during the action to denote the passage of time.

Directed by Donald McWhinnie
Designed by Hutchinson Scott

ACT ONE

SCENE I

It is a summer night.
The DELFONTS *live in a house overlooking the Regent's Canal, and the whole play takes place in the living-room and on the adjoining terrace.*
CHARLIE *is writing at a desk.*
CATHERINE *enters from the terrace, through the French windows.*

CATHERINE. Where's Leonora? . . .

CHARLIE. She's gone to bed.

CATHERINE. I wanted her to come and look at the canal.

CHARLIE. Well, she's gone to bed.

CATHERINE. I thought she might like to look at the water as it isn't term-time. I quite see that during term a thing like the Regent's Canal would be an idea to Leonora, it would be a geographical and historical and sociological idea, but during vacation I do think Leonora ought to take a look at reality. Are you listening, Charlie?

CHARLIE. Yes, Catherine.

CATHERINE. What was I saying?

CHARLIE. Leonora ought to take a look at reality.

CATHERINE. During the vacation.

CHARLIE. In the vacation.

CATHERINE. That's all I ask. I quite see that when she's in college she can't go and look at a thing without feeling compelled to go and look it up, and consequently she

I

doesn't look at things at all. But in the holidays I feel she ought to take more interest in life.

CHARLIE. The leopard can't change its spots.

CATHERINE. But Leonora isn't a leopard, that's my point. Human beings can change their spots, that's my point. Do you realise, Charlie, that all last term I didn't have a minute to look at the stars. Off to school in the morning, back in the afternoon to see what was going on in the house, homework in the evening, coaching the special boys on Saturdays, honestly I haven't looked at the stars.

CHARLIE. You can look at the stars in the holidays and in the term as well from now on.

CATHERINE. I'm not going to give up my job.

CHARLIE. I'm out of pocket with your job. I've always been out of pocket with your jobs. Extra help in the house, extra cigarettes, extra drinks to cheer you up, taxi-fares on the days when you have a row with the Head, extra clothes to maintain your authority over the boys. Extra . . .

CATHERINE. Extra ink in my fountain pen. Shoe-leather, you've forgotten shoe-leather.

CHARLIE. Extra shoe-leather. I'm out of pocket.

CATHERINE. If you get your new appointment you'll be able to afford my luxurious job in a grammar school. I have a mind as well as you and Leonora, Charlie.

CHARLIE. You can give free lectures to the Mothers' Union, it would be cheaper in the long run. I can't count on any new appointment.

CATHERINE. When will you know?

CHARLIE. Within a week or two. It's very doubtful. Don't start buying anything, just go on looking at the stars and the canal, I pay for them with the rates.

CATHERINE. Were you thinking of coming to bed or is your time too expensive?

CHARLIE. As to that, perhaps not on the whole. But I've got to finish this tonight, so clear off.

> *The scene fades out.*
> *It is later in the same evening.* CHARLIE *is still at his place.* LEONORA, *wearing a dressing-gown, enters by the door and stands behind* CHARLIE, *who does not look up from his work until she speaks.*

CHARLIE. What's the matter?

LEONORA. It isn't Catherine.

CHARLIE. Oh, it's you, Leonora. What's——

LEONORA. Charlie, give me a child.

CHARLIE. What?

LEONORA. A child, I want a child.

CHARLIE. Which child, what——?

LEONORA. I wish to conceive a child.

CHARLIE. Leonora, are you feeling all right?

LEONORA. No, because I want a child. Before it's too late. I want——

CHARLIE. Leonora. You've been overworking.

> *The scene fades out.*
> *It is the next morning, and now one sees the room from a different angle, and out, beyond the terrace, to the canal.* CHARLES *and* CATHERINE *are in the room.*

CATHERINE. It is you, Charlie, who've been overworking. I know what it is, you sit there at night and——

CHARLIE. I'm not the imaginative type, Catherine. You are always saying so. Look — I sat here. She stood there——

CATHERINE. Why didn't you call me then, why didn't you wake me up? You're always waking me up to discuss something or other. Why didn't——

CHARLIE. I was stunned. I was embarrassed. I just lay awake and thought about it.

CATHERINE. I think it was a dream. I mean to say, when you think of Leonora, when you just think of Leonora, I mean to say, Charlie. I can't think of Leonora standing here in her nightdress and saying——

CHARLIE. Her dressing-gown. Be perfectly fair.

CATHERINE. After all, if I don't know my own cousin, I mean, Charlie, we grew up together. Leonora's not that type. She's a *born* virgin. I ought to know. One always had to be very careful what one said to Leonora.

CHARLIE. That's the dangerous type.

CATHERINE. You've never thought her dangerous before.

CHARLIE. That makes her more dangerous now.

CATHERINE. No-one would believe that a university teacher like Leonora——

CHARLIE. That makes her more dangerous than ever. Remember Sarah Desmond.

CATHERINE. Who?

CHARLIE. Senior lecturer in comparative religions. The author of *The Life Force*. Life. Force. She was discovered in the bath with a wine waiter in a Folkestone hotel. It was hushed up, but she had to resign. What's more they were both naked.

CATHERINE. Leonora doesn't teach the Life Force. Greek is a very different thing from the Life Force, Greek is an old sound subject.

CHARLIE. It comes to the same thing in a woman scholar. Once they break out, they break out.

CATHERINE. I've got as good a degree as Leonora has, and I don't go round inviting men to give me a child.

CHARLIE. You've got a daughter of sorts and you've got a good husband. When will Leonora be back from her walk?

> MRS. S. *comes in with a carton from which she lifts various garments as* CHARLIE, *at the same time, places various papers in his brief-case.*

CATHERINE. She's usually back by half past ten. Where are you going? You mustn't leave me alone with her.

MRS. S. What you want to throw this away for?

CATHERINE. I've finished with it, Mrs. S. You can keep it if you like.

MRS. S. And what you want to throw this away for?

CHARLIE. I couldn't face her.

CATHERINE. Well, Charlie, neither can I, in a way.

CHARLIE. I'm glad to hear it.

CATHERINE. Although, of course, it's incredible.

MRS. S. A good vest, what's wrong with it?

CATHERINE. It got shrunk in the laundry.

MRS. S. It would come in for Daphne. She's filling out.

CATHERINE. She doesn't wear vests. Charlie, you're a rat.

> CHARLIE *is putting more things in his brief-case.*

MRS. S. Yes she does. She wears a vest in the winter when she isn't going out with a boy.

CATHERINE. Not her father's vests. Charlie, you aren't going to your club, are you?

CHARLIE. Yes I am, I'm getting out of this till you've sorted things out.

MRS. S. It'll do nicely for my niece's husband that is to be. It's his build, but of course he's young. But on the other hand, of course, he's fussy, so he might decline. She says he can't have children, I said how does he know if he hasn't had a bash at it? He must have done. She says the doctors can tell. Well you're damn lucky then, I said, in one sense, but you watch out for him in the psychological sense.

CATHERINE. It was going to be my birthday today, Charlie.

CHARLIE. It was your birthday last week.

MRS. S. Charlie was out of pocket over it, unless my ears deceived me.

CATHERINE. A rat. I was saving up my birthday for Daphne.

CHARLIE. I'll ring you after lunch. Ask her if she's ever walked in her sleep before.

MRS. S. If they walk in their sleep they don't talk in their sleep. She walked and she talked as far as I've made it my business to gather. It's nerve-wracking, Mrs. D., as between one scholar and another scholar. Charlie's not cut out for it.

> CHARLIE *goes out.*

> *She sits down and points to another chair.*

Take a seat. Rest yourself.

CATHERINE. Mrs. S., can you put all those things somewhere out of the way? Daphne will be home before lunch and Mrs. Wood will be here after lunch.

MRS. S. Oh, Annie Wood's coming, is she? You didn't tell me Annie was coming. Well that puts a different complexion on things, doesn't it? That just about puts the tin hat on it, doesn't it? What you want to invite Annie for?

CATHERINE. She rang and invited herself last night. Mrs. S., would you mind clearing away——?

MRS. S. Well, you'll have to keep your eye on Charlie. Need I elaborate on the subject?

CATHERINE. I'm not in a sociable mood this morning, Mrs. S., if you don't mind.

MRS. S. Have a fag.

She helps herself to a cigarette.

Annie hasn't got her Ph.D. like you and Leonora, has she?

CATHERINE (*examines a parcel which lies on a table*). What's this parcel?

MRS. S. Annie hasn't got her Ph.D. and that's enough for me. Charlie wants watching with women that haven't got their Ph.D's. They go to his head.

CATHERINE. What's this parcel? It's got 'For Catherine' written on it.

MRS. S. Go on, open it. It's Leonora's birthday present. You made a mistake, Mrs. D., getting your Ph.D. as a girl and then getting married to another Ph.D. Go on, open it. It's like what they do unnatural among families, the appropriate term escapes me.

CATHERINE. Incest.

Puts the parcel on top of high book-shelf.

MRS. S. Yes, shocking. And to put the lid on it you send young Daphne away to get done.

LEONORA *comes in.*

With a house full of them, you better watch out for Charlie when Annie comes. He never feels out of pocket with Annie.

LEONORA. Good morning, Catherine.

CATHERINE. Good morning, Leonora.

LEONORA. Good morning, Mrs. S.

MRS. S. To continue the subject. I wouldn't trust an eleven-plus never mind a Ph.D. Good morning, Leonora. Go and get some coffee while I finish settling the throw-outs with Mrs. D. It's warming up on the stove.

LEONORA *goes out.*

CATHERINE. Well, let's have a look, Mrs. S. Let's just take our time.

MRS. S. Perhaps as you say we're in a bit of a hurry this morning. I'll leave it for now and go and see what she's doing with the coffee. She might bring it to a boil. Fatal.

CATHERINE. No, stay here. Don't go.

MRS. S. *takes the parcel down from the book-case and puts it back on the table.*

MRS. S. You don't want to hurt Leonora's feelings. Go on, open it.

CATHERINE. No, I'm too busy just now.

MRS. S. I suppose it's a bed-jacket. It doesn't look like a book, I say it doesn't feel like a book, Mrs. D., it feels like a frilly ladies' bed-jacket, or a nightdress. It might be a quilted nylon——

LEONORA *returns with the coffee on a tray.*

MRS. S. There was iced coffee if you wanted it, but you didn't say. Go on, Mrs. D., open it.

CATHERINE. I'm too busy just now. I'll open it this afternoon when I have my birthday. Did you sleep well, Leonora?

LEONORA. Yes, what's the matter?

LEONORA *puts the parcel back on the book-case.*

MRS. S. I'll take this lot out of the way.

CATHERINE. No, Mrs. S., I always like to make time for you during the holidays and show consideration. Leonora, Mrs. S. and I have been having a deep chat. Daphne will be here before lunch. Annie's coming today, did I tell you Annie was coming, Leonora? Charlie had to rush off for some reason. Mrs. S. has discovered a delightful vest amongst these old clothes.

MRS. S. *places the carton aside.*

MRS. S. Oh no, Mrs. D., oh no. If you're going to come to a climax, this is no place for me. After six years going on seven in an academic household I've learned to preserve my detachment and scholarly calm on the other side of the door.

She goes out.

LEONORA. Want some?

CATHERINE. Yes, if it's hot.

LEONORA *gives* CATHERINE *her coffee and opens the newspaper.*

Of course, Leonora, the news is vitally absorbing today. I've only had time to look at the headlines myself, but they look too exciting for words — 'Three Turkish Leaders Arrested', 'I Withdraw Ban, says Bishop', 'Car Crash Death Toll', 'Warning to West'. Whatever shall we be hearing next?

LEONORA. What's wrong?

CATHERINE. Nothing. I feel a bit intense because it's my birthday. Shifting it from last week to this was a great mistake.

LEONORA. There's a little something from me in that parcel up there.

CATHERINE. I'm going to open it later, Leonora, when I've more time to enjoy the surprise. I thought it would be nice when Daphne comes and we can cut the cake. Annie's coming too. Did you know Annie was coming?

LEONORA. Yes, I took the telephone call last night.

CATHERINE. So you did. We'll be quite a family, Leonora. Did you happen to hear a noise in the night by any chance?

LEONORA. No, why? Have you been burgled?

CATHERINE. Oh, I forgot actually to thank you for your present, Leonora. I mean, of course I intend to thank you properly when I open it. But thank you now, in advance. Thank you very much indeed, it's sweet of you to remember. Charlie had to rush off, what a pity.

LEONORA. Pull yourself together, Catherine.

CATHERINE. I think I'm more together than you are. Were you disturbed by anything at ten past one this morning? Did you get up for any reason?

LEONORA. No. Why?

CATHERINE. Charlie fell asleep at his work. He had a peculiar dream, a dream.

LEONORA. What makes you think I would be disturbed by Charlie's dreams? Did he call out?

CATHERINE. No, he didn't. That's what I can't make out, because you entered into his dream.

LEONORA. I'm not responsible for Charlie's dreams.

CATHERINE. He was accosted. I thought perhaps it might not have been a dream. But I see now that it was a dream. I apologise.

LEONORA. I accept your apology.

CATHERINE. It seems odd that you should accept an apology for an offence of which you don't know the nature or the details.

LEONORA. I can imagine the nature and the details.

CATHERINE. It must console you in the absence of the reality.

LEONORA. Catherine, do you think I've never had an opportunity to sleep with a man?

CATHERINE. Not for a long time.

LEONORA. Why do you think so?

CATHERINE. Because of your manner and expression.

LEONORA. You're in no position to judge on that point. Obviously, my manner and expression would be very different if I were about to sleep with a man from what they are sitting here drinking warmed-up coffee with you.

CATHERINE. A woman of opportunities wears a certain manner and expression all the time, Leonora. I don't say you look your age, it's just the manner and——

LEONORA. I'm not yet old enough to look my age. I could still bear a child.

CATHERINE. I see.

LEONORA. If I should wish to do so.

CATHERINE. You need more than the wish.

LEONORA. I'm speaking theoretically.

CATHERINE. So am I, because you would need the man. Or a test-tube if you didn't want to change your manner and expression.

LEONORA. I think you're absolutely vile.

    MRS. S. *comes in to remove the tray.*

MRS. S. Flowers for Annie. How long's Annie going to stop for? My feet won't stand it. I hope this is the last lot that comes to the door.

B

CATHERINE. A fortnight I expect.

MRS. S. She'll be out on the canal with Charlie, wait and see. Dressed in her clothes. He'll linger out there with her all afternoon, showing a bad example.

CATHERINE. He can linger all night with her if he likes.

MRS. S. How long's Leonora going to stop for?

LEONORA. I'm leaving right away, Mrs. S.

CATHERINE. No, Leonora, you are not leaving right away. I'm upset.

MRS. S. Let me know when you've worked it out because of the lunch.

Goes out.

CATHERINE. You mustn't leave, Leonora. I apologise.

LEONORA. I reject your apology.

CATHERINE. Did you come down here in the night and ask Charlie to give you a child?

LEONORA. No.

CATHERINE. He says you did.

LEONORA. He must have had a dream. It's very sensational. I crave to hear more.

CATHERINE. Leonora, sometimes you bring out the very worst in me.

LEONORA. I think you must be right.

CATHERINE. Charlie is convinced that it happened. He thinks you must be suffering from a nervous disorder. It was embarrassing for Charlie.

LEONORA. It's embarrassing for me.

MRS. S. *puts her head round the door.*

MRS. S. Daphne's boy friend on the 'phone. Coming this afternoon.

CATHERINE. Did he want to speak to me?

MRS. S. No, he wanted not to speak to you. (*Withdraws.*)

CATHERINE. Daphne's boy friend is rather shy. He's called Charlie and we call him young Charlie to distinguish him from Charlie.

LEONORA. What does he do?

CATHERINE. Nuclear physics. He's just finished his postgraduate course and got a job, it's very hush-hush.

LEONORA. Is it a serious affair?

CATHERINE. I incline to think so. There have been several. But of course she must wait till she's got her degree.

LEONORA. That would be a pity. She ought to get married soon.

CATHERINE. You spoke very differently when I got married to Charlie. You opposed it.

LEONORA. You were a first-rate scholar. Daphne is no scholar at all. If she's in love with the man, she'll have a settled married life. She might take a job. in a grammar school. There will be no conflict, as there is in your case.

CATHERINE. I have a satisfactory married life as married lives go. You know nothing of married life.

LEONORA. What about your intellectual life?

CATHERINE. It's satisfied by teaching at the Grammar School.

LEONORA. I don't believe it.

CATHERINE. Why not?

LEONORA. When you come up to visit me in college you have a hankering look. I feel sorry for you at those times. I think perhaps it stabs you — the knowledge that you had it in you to become a distinguished scholar — and have become merely the mother of an average student and the wife of a second-class scholar.

CATHERINE. You needn't feel sorry for me. Charlie's one of the best economists in the country.

LEONORA. That doesn't prove him to be a first-class one.

CATHERINE. Your standards were always too high, Leonora. Reality forces one to lower one's standards. In your remote life you know nothing of reality.

LEONORA. I think you hanker after my remote life. I think you desire a form of reality where your standards can be high without discomfort.

CATHERINE. I might return to scholarship one day.

LEONORA. After all these years? A scholar needs continuity, Catherine.

CATHERINE. I haven't been entirely idle for all these years. I could pick up the threads if I should wish.

LEONORA. You need more than the wish, you need the capacity.

CATHERINE. What makes you think I haven't got the capacity?

LEONORA. Your manner and expression.

CATHERINE. If I sat down to study a subject, Leonora, I would have a studious look. Naturally I don't look the scholar when I'm running the house and running Charlie and correcting the fourth-form homework.

LEONORA. A woman of intellectual capacity has a certain manner and expression all the time. They are the manner and expression of detachment, and you can't pick them up overnight.

CATHERINE. I wouldn't want to pick them up at all. I like to please men. Do you think it pleases a man when he looks into a woman's eyes and sees a reflection of the British Museum Reading Room? I don't envy your expression and your manner.

LEONORA. I think you do. Sometimes you look at me like a jealous woman.

CATHERINE. That's a curious observation, considering you are so detached. In fact, I only want to know what makes you tick when I look at you.

LEONORA. What conclusion have you reached?

CATHERINE. That you're in love with something without needing it to love you back. That's how you look and act. Sometimes it's terrifying.

LEONORA. And sometimes fascinating.

CATHERINE. Yes . . . of course I'm attached to you. Don't you get tired of practising detachment?

LEONORA. I admit sometimes I get tired of being treated as a scholar and a gentleman.

CATHERINE. You ought to have got married, Leonora, if only for the pleasure of pleasing a man. Hundreds of women academics are married these days. They teach in the universities, run their homes, have babies, write books and feed their husbands — I don't know how they do it all.

LEONORA. I know how they do it all.

CATHERINE. How?

LEONORA. Badly.

MRS. S. *comes in.*

MRS. S. You got nothing done this morning, Mrs. D. It's always the same in the holidays when Leonora's here, you sit arguing the toss and nothing gets done.

CATHERINE. In our way, we've been making progress, Mrs. S.

MRS. S. In my way, I've been making the beds, Mrs. D.

LEONORA. I made my bed.

MRS. S. You didn't.

LEONORA. Didn't I? How very odd. I usually do.

CATHERINE. Perhaps you were a bit distracted this morning, Leonora?

MRS. S. Back to where we started. You better do something.

CATHERINE. What do you want me to do? I don't feel up to much. Leonora, why did you forget to make your bed?

LEONORA. I have no idea. I'm only an absent-minded professor. You could open my parcel, Catherine, if you want something to do.

CATHERINE. I'm saving it till this afternoon.

MRS. S. Go on. Open it and get it over.

    MRS. S. *gets down the parcel.*

CATHERINE. Can I trust you, Leonora?

LEONORA. What do you mean?

CATHERINE. Is it something insulting?

LEONORA. No.

CATHERINE. Mrs. S., where are the scissors?

LEONORA. Untie it. It's easy.

CATHERINE. I want scissors. Kindly allow me to organise my own home in my own way. Mrs. S. — scissors, please.

MRS S. They'll need finding.

    Goes out.

LEONORA. The situation between us is very unhealthy, Catherine.

CATHERINE. What do you mean?

LEONORA. I mean that you're so anxious about my present. I've never given you an insulting present. Really, I must leave this house.

CATHERINE. No, Leonora. I don't want you to go. I'm upset.

    MRS. S. *comes in with scissors.*

It's so exciting, opening a parcel.

MRS. S. Think it was a bomb, the way you was going on. I suppose it's a bed-jacket. Now take it easy, Mrs. D.

CATHERINE (*holds up nightdress*). It's a nightdress. A beautiful transparent feminine honeymoon nightdress.

MRS. S. That's torn it. Take a seat, Mrs. D.

LEONORA. If you don't like it, I'll keep it for myself and buy you something else.

CATHERINE. A sexy little, seductive little . . . Thank you, Leonora. You always give me something suitable for bed. Well, I suppose one spends a lot of one's life in bed, so it's quite a good idea. Nobody ever gives me a book, for instance, because it wouldn't be sensible. They know very well I haven't got time to read any book, except classics prescribed for the fourth form, even if I had the capacity to read one. I suppose you realise, Leonora, that if I had cared to make a career of scholarship I would have been a far better palaeographist than you are a classicist.

MRS. S. Leonora, if you done this on purpose, you'll get a judgment on you.

LEONORA. Catherine, I'm appalled. Tell me what book you would like to have and give me back the nightdress. It's the sort of thing I like to wear myself.

CATHERINE (*tossing the nightdress on top of the box of old clothes*). You may add it to your niece's trousseau, Mrs. S.

MRS. S. There's a way to give, Mrs. D., and a way not to give. However, I make allowance for the conflict raging at present within you between your Ph.D. that was and the nuptial significance of the nightie in question.

LEONORA. This is a pathetic fuss, Catherine. I didn't realise you were quite so touchy on the subject. You should have a holiday.

CATHERINE. I should never have got married, Leonora. You were right. It was a mistake.

LEONORA. You could not have stood a celibate life. You would always have been divided.

CATHERINE. I'll tell you where I made the mistake. Marriage — yes. But I shouldn't have married into the academic world. Can you imagine what it has felt like, as a scholar, to be the mere chattel of another scholar for all these years?

LEONORA. You exaggerate. Charlie doesn't treat you like a chattel. You've had a very pleasant life.

CATHERINE. I shouldn't have married Charlie. In some ways it was unfair to Charlie. I should have married a stockbroker. I should have married a bank manager, or a butcher or a baker. I had to have my sex, and my child, but I should have married someone who wouldn't eat up my brain, my mind. I should have married an electrician, a plumber. I should have married a hulking great LORRY DRIVER.

Enter DAPHNE *followed by* CHARLIE BROWN, *hulking great lorry driver.*

DAPHNE. Hallo, Mother. I got a lift on a lorry. I've asked the driver in for a cup of tea.

CATHERINE. Oh !

DAPHNE. Let me introduce . . . what's your name ?

CHARLIE B. Just call me Charlie, we're all called Charlie.

DAPHNE. Mother, Leonora, this is Charlie. Where's Mrs. S. ? We want a cup of tea, don't we, Charlie ?

CHARLIE B. Lot a books you got.

CATHERINE. Perhaps Charlie would be more comfortable in the kitchen with Mrs. S. She has tea brewing all day long.

DAPHNE. Certainly not. Sit down, Charlie. I'm very grateful to Charlie, he's saved me a train journey, not to mention the fare, and given me a most amusing morning. Charlie, do tell that story about the professor's wife you gave a lift to who made a pass at you. I'll go and get you some of Mrs. S.'s tea. Does anyone else want some ?

Exit.

LEONORA. Not on top of that foul coffee.

CATHERINE. We shall try to improve our standards in future.

CHARLIE B. You got a guest house here ?

CATHERINE. More or less.

CHARLIE B. Lot of books you got. I got a book at home, might interest you.

LEONORA. Goodness, the time ! I have to be off.

CATHERINE. Leonora, you're not leaving?

LEONORA. I'm only going to the British Museum.

CATHERINE. What are you doing at the British Museum?

LEONORA. Research.

DAPHNE *comes in with* CHARLIE BROWN'S *tea.*

DAPHNE. Charlie, it's my mother's birthday today. Actually it was last week but we decided to hold it today. She doesn't look her age, does she?

CHARLIE B. No. (*To* CATHERINE) You must a been a nice-looking woman.

DAPHNE. I've got a present for you in my case, Mother.

CATHERINE. What sort of research are you doing, Leonora?

LEONORA. Assyrian palaeography. I have to be off——

CATHERINE. But that was my subject. It was my subject.

LEONORA. You didn't exhaust it. I've been doing this for two years, I'm writing a short book — only a monograph.

CATHERINE. I don't see why you can't stick to Greek. I don't see why you want to dabble in my subject.

Exit LEONORA.

I'll leave you to look after Charlie. I've got nothing done this morning. Perhaps Charlie needs to be off, if he's had his tea.

CHARLIE B. No, I'm not in any hurry. Plenty time.

MRS. S. *comes in.*

MRS. S. You go and unpack your things, Daphne.

DAPHNE. Thanks for the lift, Charlie, anyhow.

Exit.

MRS. S. You finished your tea?

CHARLIE B. Yes thanks.

MRS. S. Well I better clear away, then. It's gone twelve — I suppose you want to be off.

CHARLIE B. No, I'm in no hurry. If it isn't your own time you might as well relax. Lot a books. Have they read them all?

MRS. S. They don't use them for reading, they are educated people, they refer to them. You better get off. The old father might come in and find you.

CHARLIE B. Oh, I'm used to that. Funny sort of guest house, this.

MRS. S. 'This is the home, situated near Regent's Park, of the celebrated economist, Charles Delfont and his charming wife and daughter who is at present doing a post-graduate course in sociology at Oxford. Mrs. Delfont, before her marriage a scholar in her own right, told *Life and Looks* that she has found it perfectly easy to reconcile her capacity for intellectualism with the duties of wife and mother. "After all," she said with a serene smile, "higher education broadens the horizons, and is especially helpful to married relations when one's husband is also a bit of an egg-head." At present she has a job — teaching boys in a grammar school. "It helps to keep the pot boiling," said Mrs. Delfont, an eminently practical woman in spite of her learned background.'

CHARLIE B. I don't follow your drift.

MRS. S. It was all in *Life and Looks* journal.

CHARLIE B. Remarkable memory you got.

MRS. S. If you'd a been here the day that *Life and Looks* came for the interview you'd a remembered it too. I been here six years. It's been an education in itself. Nice people. No television.

CHARLIE B. Bit unnatural, that.

MRS. S. They don't take no notice of natural and unnatural. Experienced people. They get a bit Freudian at times, of course, but it all comes out in the wash. Now you get out of here quick. Annie's coming this afternoon.

CHARLIE B. Who?

MRS. S. Cousin Annie.

CHARLIE B. That's funny. I got a sister called Annie.

MRS. S. Our Annie is a person of means, of glamour and also of democratic instincts.

CHARLIE B. I'll keep that in mind. Ta-ta.

MRS. S. Au revoir.

CURTAIN

END OF SCENE

ACT ONE

SCENE II

The same, in the afternoon.
DAPHNE *and* CHARLIE.

DAPHNE. An enormous scene, just because I gave her a nightdress. It cost thirty-seven and six. She gave it away to Mrs. S. She'll have to see a psychiatrist.

CHARLIE. You just mind your own business and leave your mother's neurosis alone. She's had it as long as I've known her, and if it's good enough for me it's good enough for you. It's a damned ridiculous present, in any case, to bring home to your mother. A nightdress!

DAPHNE. It's a perfectly normal present for a normal woman.

CHARLIE. Yes, but I'm talking abour your mother. And remember your grant doesn't extend to giving birthday presents at the price of thirty-seven and six. It's got to come out of my pocket, that thirty-seven and six. If you'd got her a book it would have been eighteen and six at the most, less thirty-three and a third per cent discount through the trade. If you'd come to me I could have got you an interesting book for your mother for twelve and fourpence. Plus postage and packing. Tenpence at the outside. Instead of which, what do you do? You sail into some exclusive shop and order a nightdress at ⁺thirty-seven and six. If you'd got your mother a book on the other hand, you would have saved me close on twenty-five shillings and your mother a fit. And when you consider the question that the book could have been set off against tax . . .

DAPHNE. I wish I had normal parents.

CHARLIE. I didn't have normal parents, why should you have normal parents? My father was a Tory and my mother believed in God. I couldn't bring my friends home. You've got it easy, my girl, compared with me.

DAPHNE. Your parents sound marvellous to me. I've got Charlie Weston coming to tea this afternoon. Suppose he takes it into his head to bring her a nightdress?

CHARLIE. He's only met her twice.

DAPHNE. Yes, but one never knows. And then there would be a scene. And then I could never face Charlie again because he would know the sort of stock I came from.

CHARLIE. You know she doesn't make scenes in front of strangers, don't exaggerate.

DAPHNE. She would make a worse scene with us after he'd gone.

CHARLIE. Is he likely to arrive here with a nightdress in his hand? I'm asking you as a girl whose faculty of reasoning I've spent a fortune on. If it seems probable to you, who have had the opportunity to observe Weston's social instincts, that he's likely to offer his hostess the gift of a nightdress, then I don't want his sort here.

DAPHNE. I have been over twenty-one for some time, Father.

CHARLIE. So have I. It's been a heavy responsibility. Have you seen Leonora today by any chance?

DAPHNE. I can choose my own friends. I could leave home if I wanted. Chuck my studies. Take a job . . .

CHARLIE. Have you seen Leonora today?

DAPHNE. Only for a few moments after I arrived. She went off to the British Museum. She wasn't here for lunch.

CHARLIE. Did you notice anything unusual about her?

DAPHNE. No.

Enter CATHERINE.

CATHERINE. Daphne, it's just occurred to me, does that young man of yours know it's my birthday?

DAPHNE. Yes.

CATHERINE. Well, you shouldn't have told him. He might bring me a present. I'm sure he can't afford it. It's appallingly bad manners to mention birthdays.

DAPHNE. Perhaps he'll forget.

CATHERINE. Perhaps he won't.

DAPHNE. He's hardly likely to give you a nightdress, now is he?

CATHERINE. Daphne dear, I have nothing against a nice nightdress, but Leonora gave me a nightdress as well.

CHARLIE. How did you find Leonora this morning?

CATHERINE. As usual.

CHARLIE. Did you talk to her at all?

CATHERINE. I did nothing else.

CHARLIE. How did it go?

CATHERINE. As usual. First I got the upper hand, then she got the upper hand, only more so. In the end, I had to admit that my marriage was a failure. I should have had a fellowship and a lorry driver instead.

DAPHNE. What's happened to Leonora?

CHARLIE. It didn't happen to Leonora, it happened to me. I was the victim. She came down in her dressing-gown last night, stood by my chair, and asked me to give her a child. Just like that — 'Give me a child, I want a child'. The woman's ill.

DAPHNE. What an amazing happening! — Leonora's so unapproachable.

CHARLIE. I didn't approach her. She——

CATHERINE. She denied it absolutely this morning.

CHARLIE. Denied it?

CATHERINE. Absolutely.

DAPHNE. This is not a normal house.

CHARLIE. I suppose it was to be expected that she'd deny it.

DAPHNE. Could she have been walking in her sleep?

CHARLIE. I suppose it is possible.

CATHERINE. Could you have been dreaming, Charlie?

CHARLIE. I wasn't dreaming, Catherine.

CATHERINE. She seemed just as sane as ever.

DAPHNE (at window). Here she is.

CHARLIE. What shall I say?

CATHERINE. Behave as if nothing had happened. Perhaps nothing did happen.

CHARLIE. I wasn't dreaming, Catherine.

CATHERINE (slightly louder voice). Hallo, Leonora. Did you have a good day at the British Museum?

LEONORA. I didn't have a day. But with what was left of the day I managed to get something done. I'm coming to the end of my book. It's a very satisfying feeling to be coming to the end of a detailed study after two years.

DAPHNE. What's the subject?

CATHERINE. Assyrian palaeography.

DAPHNE. Wasn't that your subject?

CATHERINE. Yes, but it's anyone's subject who has the ability, and the solitude and the freedom, and the leisure and the will to study the ancient writings of the Assyrians. As you know, I've never had the time and the freedom and the . . .

DAPHNE. I wish anyone joy of Assyrian palaeography. It's a dead end. It's absurd. (*Goes out.*)

LEONORA. What's the matter with her?

CHARLIE. Moral arrogance. She's been insufferable since she was arrested with Bertrand Russell.

LEONORA. The more I see of her generation the happier I am that I have no children. Charlie, what was this extraordinary dream you had about me last night? Catherine reproached me bitterly this morning with making improper advances to you in the dead of the night.

CATHERINE. Leonora, I was only saying what Charlie——

CHARLIE. Leonora, I suppose it must have been in a dream. I decided it must be so the moment you came in, just now. I must have fallen asleep in my chair. And yet, it was extremely realistic. I'm sorry. It's embarrassing. Please forget it.

CATHERINE. Charlie's been working too hard. Charlie you know you have, that's what I told you when——

LEONORA. I rather resent being dreamt about by a fellow scholar, let alone being accused of accosting him by his wife. Unconsciously you must both disrespect me.

CATHERINE. All right, I apologise, Leonora. (*Going out.*) I apologise for my existence, for having been born to accuse you of something normal like wanting a child. Charlie apologises, too . . . (*Exit.*)

CHARLIE. I apologise, Leonora.

c

LEONORA. I accept your apology. (*Opens book.*)

CHARLIE. I'm really sorry. I wish I could convey the realism. It was an interesting experience, Leonora.

> LEONORA *continues reading.*
> *Car draws up outside.*

That's probably Annie. (*Jumps up and goes to window. Returning and picking up newspaper.*) No, it isn't Annie, it's Daphne's young man.

> LEONORA *reads on.*

Daphne's boy friend. Charlie's his name.

> LEONORA *goes on reading.*

If she marries him I'm going to insist on being called Charles to avoid confusion.

> LEONORA *goes on reading.*

Damn fool if she marries him. He's empty. Can't open his mouth. He must be empty or he wouldn't want to marry her. If she wasn't such a fool she would see that. (*Turns to crossword.*) Someone's started it.

> LEONORA *leans back, closes her eyes as if tired, rests head on the chair.* CHARLIE *closes the door, goes to the desk, looks at some correspondence.* LEONORA *gets up very silently and approaches* CHARLIE.

LEONORA. Charlie.

CHARLIE. Oh!

LEONORA. Give me a child. I wish to conceive a child.

CHARLIE. Look Leonora, just sit over here quietly. Everything's going to be all right. It's just . . .

LEONORA. Before it's too late, I want . . .

> *Enter* MRS. S. *with tray,* YOUNG CHARLIE *with tray, followed by* DAPHNE *and* CATHERINE.

CATHERINE ⎫ Honestly, it's a delightful surprise . . .

MRS. S.   ⎬ She was afraid it would be a bed-jacket . . .

DAPHNE   ⎭ Put it down here, Charlie.

LEONORA *returns to her chair.*

CATHERINE. Charlie, guess what Charlie brought me for my birthday! A book. A copy of Yeats' *Collected Poems*.

MRS. S. We already got Yeats' *Collected Poems*.

CATHERINE. Oh, but this is for my very own. The other copy is for household use. . . . It's awfully difficult to come by. It's the most valued present . . .

MRS. S. (*putting down tray and going to book-shelf*). What edition is it?

CATHERINE. Oh, there's only one edition, 1933.

MRS. S. (*takes down copy of* Yeats). No, there's a later edition. Ours is the 1961 edition. 1933 edition has been superseded if I might point out. Plenty available in the second-hand bookshops now.

YOUNG CHARLIE. Sorry about the wrong edition. Not my subject.

CATHERINE. I prefer this edition.

YOUNG CHARLIE. Bottle of scent would have been better. Or even a nightdre——

MRS. S. That would a torn it, young Charlie. Mrs. D. has got a mind. You can't dab a bit of scent on a mind but you can dab poetry on it. Stands to reason.

CATHERINE. This is really splendid, young Charlie. It isn't on the fourth form curriculum either. Charlie, tell young Charlie how much I've been pining for someone to give me a book. It's a symbol of respect.

CHARLIE. She has been pining.

CATHERINE. Charlie, what's the matter with you? (*Looks at* LEONORA.) You're not still quarrelling, are you? I thought you were going to make it up.

CHARLIE. Catherine, I've got to go out, I'm afraid.

MRS. S. Aren't you going to wait for Annie?

DAPHNE. We shall have tea now, Annie or no Annie. Father, you've got to stay and monopolise Annie.

MRS. S. Or else Annie will monopolise young Charlie.

CATHERINE. Charlie, don't be a bore on my official birthday. Annie will be disappointed if you aren't here for her to flirt with. Not that I mind that about Annie. Not that. But there is something that I do mind about Annie, and if she does it again this time I'm going to put her firmly in her place.

DAPHNE. What does she do?

MRS. S. Walks about on the landing in her knickers.

CATHERINE. No, it isn't that. I don't mind that. It's when she opens her mouth and starts to inform the world on a question of scholarship. She just opens her mouth and she gives forth with absolute certainty on subjects about which she doesn't know a damn. Have you noticed it, Leonora?

LEONORA. Annie certainly does get out of her depth at times.

CATHERINE. If she does it again, Leonora, will you scream?

LEONORA. I shall try to scream. Introduce me to young Charlie, please.

MRS. S. Dr. Leonora Chase, Ph.D., early edition — Dr. Charlie Weston, Ph.D., late edition.

LEONORA. Come and sit over here, young Charlie. You're doing nuclear research?

MRS. S. He won't answer. He's very hush-hush.

> *Car draws up with screech outside.*
> *Noise and bumps. Voices. Delay.*
> *Bell rings.*

That's her. (*Goes out.*)

> *More bumps.*

CATHERINE. Annie always brings a lot of luggage.

MRS. S. (*throws open door as* ANNIE *enters*). Mrs. Annie Wood, *non*-Ph.D. ! (*Withdraws.*)

ANNIE. Do you know, there was a marvellous lorry driver outside when I drove up. He helped me in with my luggage. Isn't he big? He said I could call him Charlie.

DAPHNE. That's my lorry driver !

ANNIE. I think it good that young persons should learn to share. Charles. Catherine. Leonora. Heavenly to see you looking so sane and steady and solid after the mad crazy world I live in. I always boast about my learned cousins, I tell all my friends, I say 'They are Doctors of Philosophy, every one of them. They live such dignified lives, my dears. They have stately conversations with each other. They never have to take pep-up pills or keep-calm pills. Philosophers, that's what they are.' It's perfectly true, my dears, you have philosophical hearts, that's why it's so peaceful to come amongst you. Who is this adorable-looking young man?

CATHERINE. Daphne's young friend, Charlie Weston. My cousin, Mrs. Wood. Charlie is a nuclear-physicist, Annie, he's doing secret work.

ANNIE. Really? Tell me all about it.

> YOUNG CHARLIE *smiles.*

ANNIE (*hunting in large hand-bag*). He has a most eloquent smile. Where's that . . . I've got a present for you, Catherine, but I can't . . .

CATHERINE. Oh, Annie, you shouldn't. . . . I hope . . .

ANNIE (*still hunting*). Come and sit beside me, Charlie, while I look for Catherine's present.

Both CHARLIES *move towards* ANNIE.

CATHERINE. We make a distinction between the two Charlies, Annie, by calling them young Charlie and Charlie.

ANNIE *beams at* YOUNG CHARLIE, *who sits beside her while* CHARLIE *retreats.*

CATHERINE. Charlie, what's the matter? Haven't you made it up with Leonora? I sense something.

ANNIE. Here it is. (*Hands* CATHERINE *parcel.*) I sense something too. Leonora, I've advised you before. I know you're brilliant, but if you want to keep on the right side of a man you've got to say nice things to him. There's no point in just winning a learned argument, it——

CATHERINE. This looks very exciting.

ANNIE. Don't look so worried, Catherine, it's only a book.

CATHERINE. Marler's Economical Cookery.

ANNIE. I thought you would obviously not have a cookery book in the house. It will be a change from your studies and all that heavy reading, Catherine. Something womanly.

CATHERINE. Thank you, Annie. (*Places book aside.*) Charlie — young Charlie — wouldn't you like to go and sit beside Daphne? You don't want to be stuck with us women old enough to be your mother.

YOUNG CHARLIE. No thanks.

DAPHNE. He's got a mother-fixation, quite incurable.

ANNIE. Isn't he perfectly marvellous! Now there was something I wanted to ask you, Charlie. I mean *old* Charlie. (*Fishes in large handbag.*) I've been so worried about an economic problem. I've been trying to puzzle my head, then on the way here I thought to myself 'Of course! Charlie's the man. The foremost economist in the realm. Charlie will help me.' I know I've got it here — here it is. (*Fishes out thick bank statement.*) You see, it's my bank statement. Now Charlie, look. You see that item for four and twopence? Well, it happens on every page. Look, there's two on a page. Now I never write a cheque for four and twopence. Whatever can it mean? I believe I'm being robbed.

CHARLIE. Those are charges for your cheque books. They cost four and twopence each.

ANNIE. Charlie, you're brilliant. Catherine — he's an absolutely brilliant economist. No wonder I've got an overdraft with the price of cheque books what it is. I——

MRS. S. *looks in at the door.*

MRS. S. More flowers have come for Annie. (*Withdraws.*)

LEONORA. Something's wrong with Daphne.

ANNIE. Is she allergic to the idea of pollen?

DAPHNE *dashes out, hand to mouth.* YOUNG CHARLIE *follows her.*

CATHERINE. It's my fault. We had a row before lunch about a nightdress and it's given her a stomach upset.

CHARLIE. Is that young fellow helping her to be sick in the lavatory?

CATHERINE. I suppose so. Don't interfere. We've done enough damage, Charlie.

ANNIE. What does the young man do when he's not doing his unmentionable work?

CHARLIE. Chases after my daughter. He's the quiet type. I wouldn't trust him.

ANNIE. Well, if she marries him, she'll have a marvellous life. She'll have all the say.

CHARLIE. She can't marry him. She's got to get her degree and show something for my money.

LEONORA. Daphne ought to be married, she's the marrying type. She ought to have a child.

CHARLIE *jumps up.*

CATHERINE. Instead of going on marches.

ANNIE. What's the matter, Charlie?

CHARLIE (*sitting down*). What did you say, Leonora?

LEONORA. Daphne ought to get married and have children.

CHARLIE. I thought you said a child.

LEONORA. Well, yes, for a start.

CHARLIE. I don't think you're well, Leonora.

CATHERINE. Charlie, be reasonable.

ANNIE. Charlie, you look as if you've had a frightfully bad dream.

CATHERINE. Charlie did have a curious dream last night, Annie.

CHARLIE. It wasn't a dream.

CATHERINE. Charlie, you agreed before lunch that it was. You apologised to Leonora.

CHARLIE. I know I did. (*Goes out.*)

ANNIE. Was Leonora in the dream?

LEONORA. Apparently.   It was a frightfully bad one.

ANNIE. Then it is you who should apologise to Charlie, Leonora.   I do think if one succeeds in entering a man's dreams one owes him a good dream.   How long are you staying in London?

LEONORA. Two or three weeks.   I have to go back and forward to the British Museum.

ANNIE. Haven't you finished writing your book yet?

LEONORA. What book?

ANNIE. I forget what it was called, it was a long name. Wasn't it entitled 'The Ancient Assyrians, Intimate Revelations'?

LEONORA. How do you know about my book on the Assyrians?

ANNIE. Mrs. S. told me about it a couple of years ago, when you started it.

LEONORA. How did Mrs. S. know?   I'm keeping it secret.

CATHERINE. Mrs. S. knows everything.   *I* didn't know till today.

LEONORA. Catherine, I object to Mrs. S. prying among my papers.

CATHERINE. She pries into our papers.   There isn't a thing we can do about it.   In any case, the subject is not exclusive to any one scholar.   As you know.

ANNIE. I think it awfully sad that you scholars have to spend years and years on research, and then find that all your theories are blown to hell by some new discovery.   I'm awfully sorry about these new finds in Mesopotamia, Leonora.   Two years hard labour wasted!

LEONORA. Which new finds?   What are you talking about?

CATHERINE. Oh come, Annie, now you really are out of your depths. Even I see the quarterly journals, you know.

ANNIE. I've read about it somewhere. Now where was it? I know for a fact that it blows all your theories to hell. I'm sorry, Leonora, but you'll have to begin again, right from scratch.

LEONORA. I think I would have heard of any sensational discoveries of that nature, Annie. As a matter of fact there are no excavations in progress at the moment, they hope to resume in——

ANNIE. I know where I saw it! It was in the Late Night Final. (*Fishes in hand-bag.*) Where's that paper? Here it is! Now just a minute till I find. . . . Oh yes, now listen to this: 'Sensational finds on Ancient Site: New Babylonian Writings. A young shepherd boy at Kish near the ancient site of Babylon on Tuesday narrowly escaped death by a falling boulder, and after his leap to safety noticed in the cavity revealed by the dislodged stone a number of stone tablets. Later investigation has proved that these tablets, inscribed in cuneiform characters, date back to the 5th century B.C., and apparently were the family records of a wealthy steward under Nebuchadnezzar, ranging in subject matter from the morning prayers of the household to the cost of eyepaint for concubines. "Even at a glance it is obvious that these finds are going to affect all our previous conceptions of dates, writings, customs, symbolism and religous observances of the Babylonians," said Professor G. Smart Dwight, the American Assyriologist, who——'

LEONORA. Dwight!

ANNIE. Dwight. '. . . who flew here today. Professor Dwight added, "all our previous work on Assyrian pal . . . pal . . .

CATHERINE. Palaeography.

ANNIE. '"will have to be completely revised. We shall have to start again from scratch." Professor Locking of Oxford University, who has—— '

CATHERINE. Locking!

ANNIE. Locking. '. . . of Oxford University, who has also flown to the site, confirmed this and added, "This is in the nature of a revelation. It—— " '

LEONORA. Let me see it.

CATHERINE. Let me have a look.

ANNIE. You can see it all for yourself, Leonora, in black and white. You see it blows all your theories to hell.

LEONORA *reads while* CATHERINE *looks over her shoulder.*

CATHERINE. It seems there will have to be some slight rethinking, Annie.

ANNIE. Slight re-thinking, my eye. It blows——

CATHERINE. How does it seem to you, Leonora?

LEONORA. It's exciting.

ANNIE. What do you mean, it's exciting. I blow all your theories to hell and you say it's exciting. Two years' work——

LEONORA. That doesn't matter, Annie. Forty years wouldn't matter. What matter are the new discoveries.

CATHERINE. There is a scholar's point of view, Annie, which you will never share. But we are obliged for your interesting snippet of information.

ANNIE. Well, at least I've saved Leonora another day or two's fruitless work. She's looking pale.

LEONORA. Fruitless.

ANNIE. Absolutely fruitless. If I were you, Leonora, I'd go and see a doctor, even if it's only about your health. I must go and change into something suitable for gazing across the canal by dusk. Whenever there's a gap in my life I go and see a doctor. That's *my* philosophy. (*Exit.*)

CURTAIN

END OF ACT I

ACT TWO

A week later.
Another view of the same room. French windows open. ANNIE, *dressed in an opulent dressing-gown, sits writing by a desk near the window.* CHARLIE *is in the room.*

ANNIE. Take no notice of it.

CHARLIE. I can't.

ANNIE. Well then, don't be so mean. After all, Leonora's one of the family. Give her a child if she wants a child, anything for a quiet life. How do you spell susceptible?

Enter CATHERINE *with a shopping basket.*

CATHERINE. Annie, it's gone twelve.

ANNIE. So it has. I've only written two and a half letters. Charlie has been giving me the full story of his experiences during the past week.

CATHERINE. Hadn't you better be getting dressed in case anyone comes in or something?

CHARLIE. 'Give me a child . . .'

ANNIE. I am dressed.

CATHERINE. I meant dressed in something different from your bedroom attire. Not that I myself care in the——

ANNIE. I chose this as being specially suitable for sitting by a sunny window writing letters.

CHARLIE. I don't think she knows what she's saying at the time.

39

CATHERINE. It does look rather charming, I must admit. Stand up and turn round slowly.

CHARLIE. Looks very nice, Annie. I say I don't think she knows what she's saying at the time.

CATHERINE. But I wouldn't myself call it suitable for writing letters, particularly.

ANNIE. It depends what sort of letters you write.

CHARLIE. Looks very nice, Annie—— I don't think she wants a child. It is simply something she says. She's under a compulsion to say it.

ANNIE. That's exactly what I suffer from. I'm always saying things. Something inside me makes me.

> *Enter* MRS. S.

I might easily say to you 'Charlie, give me a child, I want a child.' I mean, at the very worst you could reply, 'Anything you say, Annie darling.'

MRS. S. Did you get the cucumber, Mrs. D.?

CATHERINE. No, you didn't mention cucumber.

MRS. S. Yes, I did. — Just carry on with your conversation, Annie. — I said bring a cucumber, I could see you wasn't listening.

ANNIE. No-one would think it odd, I'm sure, if I said, 'Charlie——'

CATHERINE. Leonora's different from you, Annie.

CHARLIE. It would be a different proposition altogether, Annie.

MRS. S. Leonora hasn't got freedom of speech like you, Annie. She's educated. Daphne's on a diet to catch a husband. It wasn't much to ask, any normal mother would a laid herself out to get a cucumber under the circumstances, but I knew——

CATHERINE. Leonora's a scholar, one takes her seriously. There's no comparison, Annie, between the effect of what you might say and the effect of what Leonora says.

MRS. S. We take everything from whence it comes in this establishment, Annie. Poor Leonora don't get away with much, she can't sit around like you all morning looking like the Caliph of Bagdad's favourite Christian. Make people think she was off her rocker. You're all right, you haven't got a rocker. I wanted to slice a bit of cucumber for Daphne's salad, special diet.

CHARLIE. She should eat what's put before her.

MRS. S. Let her enjoy herself while she's young. She'll soon have her Ph.D., and once you've got it you've had it. Annie, the time's getting on if you want to change into something suitable for consuming shepherd's pie with oily lettuce leaves on your side plate.

ANNIE. Mrs. S., I'm sure Mr. S. must have loved you very dearly. I know he must have done.

MRS. S. I wouldn't be sure. I remain agnostic on that point. What makes you raise the subject, academically speaking?

ANNIE. I always like to bring the conversation round to love, I do it by instinct.

MRS. S. A pernicious instinct. Enough to spoil your appetite. (*Goes out.*)

CHARLIE. A drink, Annie, . . . Catherine . . .?

ANNIE. Yes, please — my usual.

CATHERINE. Please. Annie can take hers——

ANNIE. Annie can take it upstairs while she changes.

CATHERINE. Annie dear, do what you like. I'm all on edge.

ANNIE. I think you very calm and detached in the circumstances, Catherine.

CATHERINE. Thank you, but I don't feel it.

CHARLIE. Neither do I.

ANNIE. You don't look it. Catherine does, she's brilliantly calm.

CHARLIE. She says she does not feel it.

ANNIE. Then she has a marvellous control over her feelings.

CHARLIE. Catherine is usually controlled when she's got something to worry about, she only loses control when she's worried about nothing.

ANNIE. Are you sure you are not worrying about nothing? After all, Leonora may be having a little joke. One gets bored at times, after all, and one might easily . . .

CHARLIE. Leonora doesn't play little jokes.

CATHERINE. Her jokes are entirely academic and verbal.

ANNIE. I wonder, Charlie, if you've been imagining, or partly dreaming about Leonora? Let me assure you that one isn't morally responsible for what one dreams. A priest told me that.

CATHERINE. Annie——

Enter DAPHNE.

DAPHNE. The tape recorder's gone. Have you got it?

CATHERINE. What do you mean, it's gone?

CHARLIE. Where's it gone?

DAPHNE. Someone has taken it. Annie, have you moved a tape recorder from the broom cupboard this morning?

ANNIE. I never go near a broom cupboard, darling.

CATHERINE. Have you asked Mrs. S.?

DAPHNE. She hasn't seen it. Someone must have taken it very early this morning. I hid it in the cupboard very late last night. It's still got the tape in it.

CHARLIE. Damn silly place to put it. Why didn't you take it to your room?

DAPHNE. I thought it would be safer in the broom cupboard. I thought nobody would find it there.

ANNIE. Leonora must have found it there. Leonora's got it, obviously. Leonora's probably bored now that she hasn't got her book to write. Ask Leonora when she comes in, you'll find she's borrowed it, after all it's only a tape recorder. Is it a very high-class one?

DAPHNE. It isn't mine. I borrowed it for a purpose.

CHARLIE. I can't afford to replace it.

CATHERINE. We managed to get a recording of Leonora's voice, Annie, to prove that she does what Charlie says she does. It's on the tape, it's there when one plays it back.

ANNIE. How thrilling. You could blackmail Leonora now, I suspect she's quite well off. It wouldn't be a real crime, would it, if you just kept it in the family.

CHARLIE. How could she have suspected?

ANNIE. Leonora's a scholar, you know. Scholars are very sly, you must admit they do things very much on the sly. I once met a scholar in the train to Cardiff.

CATHERINE. Supposing Leonora should play it back, not quite knowing what it was she said? It might give her a frightful shock. I wish we hadn't thought of the tape recorder. I feel rather mean.

DAPHNE. I don't. It will force her to have treatment.

CATHERINE. From whom?

D

DAPHNE. She should be psycho-analysed.

CATHERINE. I don't see Leonora submitting to psycho-analysis. She's so inevitably bound to be more intelligent than the analyst, she'd be analysing him.

DAPHNE. Something will have to be done.

CATHERINE. Something has been done.

DAPHNE. Something more will have to be done.

ANNIE. Nonsense. We had another cousin Sarah, who used to talk to the squirrels. Nothing was ever done about her. We just put up with it—— Remember, Catherine?

DAPHNE. This is quite different. There's nothing desperately odd about talking to a squirrel.

ANNIE. These squirrels were not there. We just had to put up with it. Can't you just put up with this little freak of Leonora's, Charlie?

CHARLIE. No.

CATHERINE. It upsets Charlie.

ANNIE. It flatters him.

CHARLIE. It frightens me. What are we going to do when she comes back? That's the problem.

CATHERINE. Perhaps she won't come back.

ANNIE. Oh, she wouldn't run off with Daphne's tape recorder. It would be criminal.

CATHERINE. Leonora's a serious problem, Annie. She might not return.

ANNIE. That's what Charlie wants, isn't it? So that would be an end of the problem.

CATHERINE. It would present a worse problem.

ANNIE. I've got a brilliant idea. I know what we can do.

MRS. S. (*off*). Lunch ready.

CATHERINE. What, Annie?

ANNIE. Well, in my opinion, the best way to deal with a problem is to solve it. That's what we'll do.

MRS. S. (*off*). Lunch ready.

CATHERINE. Lunch is ready.

CURTAIN

END OF SCENE I

ACT TWO

MRS. S. *with electric polisher.*
The stage is empty and without scenery except for various pulleys and switches to adjust stage scenery and lighting, but with various coloured lights upon it.
LEONORA *comes in with a tape recorder. She sits on the stage, opens the tape recorder and starts to play it back.*

LEONORA'S VOICE (*from the machine*). Charlie, give me a child, I want a child.

CHARLIE'S VOICE. Leonora, please . . .

LEONORA'S VOICE. Charlie, before it's too late. Give me a child.

CHARLIE'S VOICE. Just sit down for a moment, Leonora. You are not well.

> *Recorded footsteps retreating.*

LEONORA. That is a recording of a conversation between me and my cousin's husband.

MRS. S. Never!

> *Switches on the polisher, which makes a humming sound, and polishes the floor of the stage with it.*

LEONORA. What do you make of it, Mrs. S.?

MRS. S. Very revealing. Get up off the floor, you'll catch a cold off it.

46

LEONORA. Mrs. S., have you ever had a nervous breakdown?

MRS. S. Yes. I shall never forget it. I had it on a Tuesday afternoon in March four years ago when Mrs. D. packed her bags to leave Charlie, but Charlie failed to return home at the anticipated hour to be left. Suspense held us both in its clammy clutch. We waited, gaunt, unspeaking, resolute, in the front hall where the shadows gathered round us in fraught mockery. Outside, a car slid like a homing egret to a swift standstill. Footsteps passed and faded relentlessly into the guesswork of another street. Silence. Fate. Footsteps again. Still no Charlie. I shall never forget it. Would you get up off the floor, Leonora? I got to polish up.

LEONORA. Mrs. S. I'm occupied. This is a discovery and it requires concentration. Shall we hear it again?

MRS. S. No, we heard it the first time. If that tape came to a head you would lose your job and so would Charlie. You got a bit of fluff on your skirt.

LEONORA. Oh, that will soon brush off. The question is, what am I going to say to them all? I shall have to think of some explanation . . .

MRS. S. You'll think something up. You'd better move that machine.

LEONORA. Reality is very alarming at first and then it becomes interesting. Are you interested in the nature of reality, Mrs. S.?

MRS. S. Very, I'm trying to give it a polish as you can see.

LEONORA *gazes at the room.*

LEONORA. The wall, the room! Where is it? What's happened?

MRS. S. I told you, Leonora, I'm getting the place ready. Have patience. I've got to work in my own time-space.

LEONORA. Mrs. S., I'm frightened. Would you mind putting this back in the broom cupboard. I just can't bear the sight of it.

MRS. S. Are you interested in the nature of reality, Leonora, or are you too frightened ?

LEONORA. I'm interested.

MRS. S. Well, there isn't any broom cupboard. Dramatic revelation.

LEONORA. I got it out of the broom cupboard this morning.

MRS. S. You did and you didn't, let's face it. The broom cupboard is a pure idea somewhere behind the scenes. There's a lot goes on behind the scenes in this house that's all pure idea. It's very alarming at first and then it becomes interesting. (*She switches off the polisher.*)

> *Enter* CHARLIE BROWN *with large piece of scenery — part of the original study set. He continues to adjust scenery by working pulleys, etc., with* MRS. S. LEONORA *watches with curiosity.*

You're late, Charlie. I've had to keep the conversation going.

CHARLIE B. Hallo, good afternoon, doctor.

LEONORA. Let me try. (*She helps to adjust a piece of scenery.*)

CHARLIE B. How's your cousin ?

LEONORA. Good afternoon, Charlie. Which one ?

CHARLIE B. The healthy one.

MRS. S. That's Annie. She's in good health. Just mind out of the way, Leonora. We'll soon have the place straight.

CHARLIE B. How's the young one ?

MRS. S. Daphne's on a diet. Makes her bad tempered. Starts laying down the law.

The room is now normal, but MRS. S. *puts final touches.*

CHARLIE B. I ask the doctor a question, I don't expect answers from you. There's a question I want to put to you, doctor. Now suppose you was me. Put yourself in my place. Thirty-six. Unmarried. Good job in transport. Plenty spare time both ends of the journey. — You got the picture?

LEONORA. Yes.

CHARLIE B. Well, you're still me, see? Now you want to settle down in life. Understand?

LEONORA. Oh, yes.

CHARLIE B. But you haven't yet found the partner that you might call of your dreams. So what do you do?

LEONORA. You wait, you have a look round, and——

CHARLIE B. Quite. You wait. You got to give up travel for a week or two and wait. So what do you do while you're waiting? I'll tell you what you do. You improve yourself.

MRS. S. Hanging round the canal watching Annie rowing the boat.

CHARLIE B. I'm consulting the doctor if you'll excuse me. Where was I?

LEONORA. You improve yourself.

CHARLIE B. You're in my shoes, remember.

LEONORA. I improve myself.

CHARLIE B. Yes, that's what you do while you wait for the right party to turn up. Now, I'm not a one for evening classes. Too old. So you borrow a couple a books.

MRS S. Off of Annie. (*Points to a gap in book-shelf.*)

CHARLIE B. I'm putting up a problem. Well, to cut a long story short, doctor, if you put yourself in my place, where you're stopping the light isn't good enough to read in bed at nights. It's in the wrong place. So what do you do? You decide to buy a reading lamp. Right?

LEONORA. An excellent idea, Charlie.

CHARLIE B. Good. Now, you get dressed in a suit, you go up the West End, to Oxford Street. Right, you go into a big shop, electrical department, and you look round and you find what you want around your price. Right? Well, it's not right. You find two or three, then you bring it down to two. You're in my shoes, remember. You got a choice of a nice vase base in apple-green, black and white, chinese blossom effect, cone-shaped shade, casts a pale-green glow, no good for reading. Or on the other hand you got a choice of a desk lamp, plain red wood base, long neck, flexible, and a small shade to protect your eyes from the naked bulb, Swedish made. Which one do you choose? If you was in your own shoes you'd choose the desk lamp every time, wouldn't you?

MRS S. Say yes, Leonora.

LEONORA. Perhaps it would be more practical for reading.

CHARLIE B. That's right, for reading. But you're in my shoes. Suppose when it comes to the push you don't like the book? You put it down and you pick up the other and you don't like that one either. A couple a days later you meet the lady of your inmost desires. Where's the desk lamp going to get you? It won't get you anywhere, will it? You be better off with the chinese style vase, cone-shaped shade, pale-green glow. It would form the beginnings of a home on any mantelpiece.

MRS. S. Try saying no, Leonora.

LEONORA. Yes, in the circumstances I would choose that, Charlie.

CHARLIE B. You're sure? You're not me now, you're the doctor. Suppose I did like the first book, and suppose I liked the second. I might become a reader, isn't that so, doctor?

LEONORA. It's quite a problem, Charlie.

CHARLIE B. Let me run over the symptoms again. Thirty-six. Unmarried. Good job in transport . . .

ANNIE *comes in dressed 'for boating on the Canal'.*

ANNIE. Leonora darling! — Oh, you've got the tape recorder, shall I put it back in the broom cupboard?

She makes a swift exit with tape recorder.

CHARLIE B. Plenty of time both ends of the journey——

MRS. S. That'll be all for today, Charlie, much obliged.

CHARLIE B. I haven't finished consulting the doctor.

MRS. S. You better go before you catch any more symptoms. (CHARLIE *hesitates.*) Mrs. D. will be in presently.

LEONORA. Sit down, Charlie. I'll try to give you some definite advice.

Enter ANNIE.

ANNIE. Well, good afternoon, Charlie. Lovely day for the canal, isn't it?

CHARLIE B. A perfect day, ma'am.

ANNIE. You're always so encouraging, Charlie.

MRS. S. That's exactly what the neighbours say when he stands on the bank and yells 'Good old Annie. Go to it, Annie.'

ANNIE. I hope the neighbours notice the improvement in my style. Rowing isn't easy, it's an art. You have to give yourself up to it. I've discovered that there's no use whatsoever in making a determined effort. You've got to relax into a sort of rhythmic trance, like this. (*Sits on the floor and makes trance-like rowing movements.*) In, out . . .

CHARLIE B. Three cheers for Annie.

ANNIE (*getting up*). You'll see what I mean much better when I take out the actual boat after tea.

MRS. S. You going out on the canal in that garb?

ANNIE. Yes, I changed. All things considered, Mrs. S., my boudoir wrap would have been unsuitable and too conspicuous, one has to think of the neighbours.

MRS. S. It's too tight round the bottom for sportswear, that's point number one. Point number two, you got to remember that this is the household of a distinguished economist and he don't want to get his name in the papers in any connection that would throw a shadow of doubt on his balanced judgment. Balance is the keynote of this house, Annie. Balance is all.

ANNIE (*makes a few rowing movements*). Am I unbalanced, Leonora?

LEONORA. I'm no judge, Annie.

MRS. S. You better give Charlie your verdict, Leonora, because I've got to see him to the door.

ANNIE. What is Charlie consulting you about, Leonora?

LEONORA. A reading lamp.

MRS. S. Get up, Charlie.

LEONORA. Sit down, Charlie.

MRS. S. Leonora, they'll all be coming in soon, and they've all been upset by you, and there's a lot to straighten up in the whole affair. In my opinion the presence of an outsider might further complicate the issue. Come on, Charlie.

LEONORA. I would prefer to complicate the issue. Stay here, Charlie. Continue to call me 'doctor'. Once a doctor, always a doctor.

ANNIE. Leonora, I think you're brilliant.

MRS. S. Well, myself, I like to see people facing the facts.

LEONORA. I've already faced the facts. Annie has put them in the broom cupboard.

ANNIE. And I don't want to hear Daphne advising Leonora to see a psychiatrist on moral grounds. One should only see a psychiatrist out of boredom. Who are these flowers from?

LEONORA. And I don't want Catherine to be understanding, and Charlie to pretend that nothing's happened, all the time watching me out of the corner of his eye.

CHARLIE B. We got to show them who's boss.

ANNIE. Charlie, you're brilliant!

LEONORA. Where are they?

MRS. S. Behind locked doors, I dare say, having a conference about you. Hold on, I'll investigate.

    Exit.

ANNIE (*unwrapping flowers*). Arum lilies. I call that a very pure idea to send. Arum lilies. Very bridal.

CHARLIE B. That brings back a lot of memories.

LEONORA. Why, Charlie? — Were you ever married?

CHARLIE B. No. But there was two Lily's in my life, Lily Donelly and Lily Pearson. I never got them out of my system, not properly. Makes me feel bad to think of them, doctor, I feel shaken.

LEONORA. I'd better analyse you immediately, Charlie. (*Charlie stretches out on the sofa.*)   That's right.

ANNIE. That's brilliant!

LEONORA. Relax and go on about Lily.

CHARLIE B. Lilys.   Plural.   They both met one night in the ladies' cloakroom of the Hammersmith Palais and started to compare what you might call notes.   Well, to cut a long story short . . .

Enter MRS. S.

MRS. S. I can't turn my back a minute to listen-in without everyone taking liberties in the home.   Get up, Charlie.

LEONORA. Lie down, Charlie.   Mrs. S., I've got to think of my timing.   Timing is very important.   Are they coming?

MRS. S. Any minute now.   Daphne says she knows a clinic where they'll do you free.   Mrs. D. says she's glad she chose marriage after all.   Charlie says that if the tape recorder isn't found, how much will he have to pay for a replacement?

ANNIE. Put him out of his misery right away, Mrs. S.   Tell him the machine is in the broom cupboard.

MRS. S. (*shouts upstairs*).   Mrs. D., I got the instrument.   It's in the broom cupboard.   Don't worry, Charlie.   I say I got the machine.

Enter CATHERINE.

CATHERINE. Where. . . . Oh Leonora, I didn't know you were in, I thought you were out. . . . What's the matter, has he fainted?

MRS. S. No noise, please.   Take your seat quietly.   The patient is just going under.

LEONORA. It's most important, Charlie, that I should know a little more about your childhood in Bermondsey.

CHARLIE B. Yes, doctor, well of course we wasn't in Bermond-sey for long. We were always on the move, my dad believed in it. Seven mouths to feed, he had to keep on the credit side of things.

LEONORA. The family moves were profitable, then?

CHARLIE B. Well, we got new credit every time.

LEONORA. Just relax and go on about Lily.

CHARLIE B. Well, that would be a story, that would.

CATHERINE. Well, it's nearly tea-time and I'm sure Charlie has had enough for one session. I must say, Charlie, you seem all right to me.

CHARLIE B. No, ma'am, that's where you're wrong. You can't judge by appearances.

ANNIE. Charlie has been visited by a trauma in the last few days. He is very perplexed about a reading lamp, not to mention a couple of Lilys. I think Leonora's doing a fine job of work on Charlie.

CHARLIE B. Hear, hear. I feel better already.

LEONORA. Tomorrow at three, then, Charlie. Don't forget to make a note first thing in the morning of anything you may have dreamt in the course of the night.

CATHERINE. Do you intend Charlie to come here for daily interviews, Leonora? Because——

LEONORA. We could rig something up on the terrace if it's a fine day and if you feel we're intruding.

CATHERINE. If you wish to use your room for professional purposes, Leonora, I have no objection. The terrace is rather public.

LEONORA. My room is rather private. And really I think we had better not discuss this problem in front of my patient. He has problems enough already. Tomorrow at three, then, Charlie. Goodbye, and whatever you do, don't worry.

CHARLIE B. Au revoir and thank you, doctor. (*Turns to* ANNIE *at door*.) I'll be watching out for you on the canal.

ANNIE. Don't forget to make a note of any points of style that you may feel need improvement, Charlie.

CHARLIE B. Yes. I got a lot a notes to make. Ta ta. (*Goes out.*)

CATHERINE (*dusting sofa where* CHARLIE B.'s *feet have been*). Why are you doing this, Leonora?

LEONORA. It's an exercise in compassion.

CATHERINE. That lorry driver doesn't need your help, Leonora. He's tough. That kind doesn't suffer from nerves.

LEONORA. I mean it's an exercise in compassion for him.

CATHERINE. Well, if that's what you mean, I don't know what you mean.

LEONORA. I mean he was sorry for me to the extent that he desired to help me.

CATHERINE. Well it seemed to me you were doing all the exercise of compassion, solving his problem. You seemed very interested in him.

LEONORA. Interest is not the same thing as compassion, you gross, crude, vulgar, bloated intellectual.

Enter CHARLIE.

CATHERINE. I am not gross, crude, vulgar and bloated.

LEONORA. What do you know of compassion?

CHARLIE. We're sorry for you, Leonora, if that's what you mean.

LEONORA. You experience the emotion of pity for me?

CHARLIE. Well, yes, if you want pity.

LEONORA. You don't seem to approve of the word.

CHARLIE. Well, pity's an embarrassing word.

LEONORA. Because it's an embarrassing emotion. Anything one has neglected is embarrassing. One hesitates to show one's pity in the same way that one would be slow to display an under-nourished animal. People would notice there was something wrong with it and that would be embarrassing.

CATHERINE. Leonora, we would like to help you somehow, and to exercise pity as you call it.

LEONORA. But you don't know how to do so.

CATHERINE. Well, no. It's a difficult problem.

LEONORA. Why? You've had twenty years to study the subject. When your marriage prevented you from continuing your studies why didn't you turn to studying the only other subject conveniently to hand? Why have you not given the same attention to the quality of your own emotions as you would have given to the quality of the handwriting of the ancient Assyrians?

CATHERINE. What have you done about your emotions, Leonora?

LEONORA. Nothing. I'm a professional scholar and I am not supposed to do anything about my emotions. You, on the other hand, have been under an obligation to do so for the past twenty years. What have you done with your time?

CATHERINE. I love my husband and my daughter, naturally.

LEONORA. So does any married woman without any intellectual distinction. Why do you find it so difficult to know what to do about me? If you had spent your time cultivating an understanding of compassion you would find it easy. What you call pity is not pity at all. Your pity is a word existing in the mind like your broom cupboard, it——

ANNIE. Would you try one of my pills, Leonora? It's got something in it that lifts you up and another thing that calms you down. It won't have any effect whatsoever. I can't do without them.

CATHERINE. I'll try one, Annie, if you don't mind.

ANNIE. You take it with water.

CHARLIE. Water, Leonora — behind you in the jug.

CATHERINE. To hell with you, Leonora, for sitting there lecturing us and putting us in the wrong.

CHARLIE. Attack is a usual form of defence.

CATHERINE. Charlie hasn't been sleeping. What pity have you got for Charlie?

LEONORA. A certain amount. But I'm not sure what kind of pity it is.

CHARLIE. I don't want anyone's pity.

Enter MRS. S. *with tea-tray, followed by* DAPHNE.

MRS. S. I been and muddled up all your papers, Leonora. They just fell to bits on the floor and the pages isn't numbered.

LEONORA. You shouldn't meddle with my work, Mrs. S. Which batch have you muddled?

MRS. S. Your new line of study.

DAPHNE. Leonora, I hope you haven't started any new work. You need a rest.

MRS. S. Entitled ' "Observations of Human Reactions to Pitiable Objects." First case history — the economist who, when put to the test of an artificial encounter——'

LEONORA. My notes are private, Mrs. S.

CHARLIE. Did you say case history of an economist?

MRS. S. I did. But I shouldn't of. Mrs. D., what have you done with the half a cucumber I put away for Daphne?

CATHERINE. I threw it out. It was dry.

DAPHNE. It wasn't dry. I'm pining for cucumber.

CHARLIE. Did you say case history of an economist, or was it a communist?

MRS. S. Economist. You think I don't know the difference?

DAPHNE. It was only dry at the end. What a waste!

MRS. S. It goes 'First case history — the economist who, when put to the test of an artificial encounter contrived by the author——'

CHARLIE. Leonora, what is the title of your thesis?

MRS. S. I told you the title. 'Observations of Human Reactions to Pitiable Objects.' (Goes out.)

DAPHNE. Have you told Leonora what you said you were going to say?

CATHERINE. No. Leonora has been having all the say.

DAPHNE. I think you're both very cowardly. Leonora, we want to ask you to consult a psychiatrist and have a course of treatment.

CHARLIE. Be careful what you say, Daphne.

CATHERINE. Why should she be careful? Leonora has not been careful what she has said.

DAPHNE. It's a simple matter of repressed emotions and desires, Leonora. These schizophrenic symptoms like

E

accosting Father with suggestions, well, they might occur again. You might approach some ancient male colleague one dark night. Next time you have an attack——

CHARLIE. Daphne, I wish you would be quiet.

DAPHNE. Someone's got to speak. Now that Leonora has found out that she was quite unconsciously making absurd remarks, she must see that something must be done.

LEONORA. My discovery was very dramatic. I suspected something, of course, but when I heard my own voice on the tape recorder, it was a kind of liberation. It felt like a cure in itself. Sometimes these revelations seem to occur in a dramatic way for curative purposes. I must say, I feel myself to be occupying a very dramatic role now. It's quite a new sensation.

ANNIE. I know exactly how you feel, Leonora. I've had a dramatic feeling all my life. It's thrilling.

DAPHNE. Once you start feeling dramatic you might do anything. You might do it at Oxford.

LEONORA. So might you.

DAPHNE. What do you mean?

CHARLIE. Daphne, it's my belief that Leonora is enacting a part simply in order to observe my reactions. The whole thing was contrived.

CATHERINE. Leonora, if you have done this to your own kith and kin——

LEONORA. I deny it. It was a humiliating experience for me, and I remain an object of your pity.

CATHERINE. You don't appear very humiliated. Quite the opposite. You've been laying down the law all afternoon. How can one exercise pity on people who are arrogant?

ANNIE. Oh, Catherine, Leonora is very humble, she has just admitted that she honestly didn't know what she was saying when she said 'Charlie, give me a——'

CHARLIE ⎱Annie, don't. Please don't repeat those words.
ANNIE   ⎰'. . . child. I want a——'

LEONORA. Charlie knows it all by heart, Annie.

CHARLIE. Leonora, I shall never know what to believe.

ANNIE. It was most dramatic.

LEONORA. It was a kind of dramatic urge. You are in a way to blame for the form it took, and so is Catherine.

CATHERINE. I knew we would be to blame in the end.

LEONORA. I have occupied the role in which you've cast me. At times of low spirits when one is tired one behaves largely as people expect one to behave. It has been expected of me that I should be envious of you, Catherine, and should want Charlie to give me a child. I've instinctively played a part in your minds of Leonora the barren virgin.

DAPHNE. Well, Leonora, isn't that the truth?

LEONORA. Not the whole truth. The definition excludes other aspects of my personality which are also true.

CATHERINE. The definition is yours, Leonora. We have never referred to you as Leonora the barren virgin. Have we, Charlie?

LEONORA. Charlie has frequently said to his daughter, 'Your maiden aunt will be here next week.'

DAPHNE. How did you know that?

CHARLIE. Daphne, be careful what you say. Leonora's preparing a thesis based on personal observations of human reactions. We shall all be in the book.

LEONORA. I am trying to point out the context in which you think of me.

DAPHNE. Of course you aren't really my maiden aunt, you're my maiden second cousin, to be accurate.

LEONORA. And even that might not be accurate.

DAPHNE. Why won't you consult a psychiatrist?

LEONORA. It would reduce me to the ranks. I'm not prepared to be reduced to the ranks, now that I have obtained such an exhilarating glimpse of my dramatic position.

ANNIE. Leonora darling, I think you're brilliant. That's exactly what I said to my C.O. in the Wrens when she was trying to intimidate me about some silly business with a lance-corporal. I said to her, 'I'm not prepared to be reduced to the ranks, that's all.' I said, 'Not when I'm having such a thrilling time up here I'm not going to be reduced to the ranks.' Of course, she knew I had the Air Vice-Marshal behind me. But it was a most dramatic moment. As soon as she mentioned the ranks I realised that I was a woman of destiny. No woman of destiny, Leonora, should permit herself to be reduced to the ranks, it would be most undramatic.

CATHERINE. I don't think I can cope with both my cousins having dramatic senses of themselves. I wish I could have a dramatic sense of myself, it must be lovely. But I'm too honest. It's stark reality for me, every time.

LEONORA. For me, it's a glimpse of reality which gives me the dramatic sense of myself. Perhaps the same applies to Annie.

CATHERINE. What sort of reality? Everyday life?

LEONORA. Not the everyday life I've known so far. But I have a definite sense of being *watched*.

DAPHNE. What?

CATHERINE. What did you say?

LEONORA. A definite sense of being observed and listened to by an audience.

CATHERINE. What sort of audience?

LEONORA. An invisible audience. Somewhere outside. Looking at all of us and waiting to see what's going to happen.

ANNIE. Leonora, this is thrilling. All my life I've had a feeling of being looked at by an audience. That's why I always take care to be suitably dressed.

LEONORA. Shall Annie consult a psychiatrist, too?

CATHERINE. Oh Annie. Annie has always been like that.

LEONORA. Well, now I'm like that. A great many dons are like that. We all go dotty in the end.

CATHERINE. I see. Somehow I thought you spoke with conviction when you mentioned a sense of being watched. It's a well-known symptom.

ANNIE. I speak with conviction.

DAPHNE. This might be the beginning of something like religious mania, Leonora. There's a type of religious mania where the patients are beset by a terrible sense of being watched. They feel eyes upon them.

LEONORA. I feel eyes upon me.

DAPHNE. It must be ghastly. At least you should see a general practitioner.

LEONORA. My condition isn't in the least distressing. It's most interesting. Exhilarating. I feel like the first woman who's ever been born. I feel I've discovered the world.

ANNIE. I know exactly how you feel, Leonora. I've never felt otherwise myself. Only I couldn't put it into words.

LEONORA. Beware of religious mania, Annie. There are eyes upon you. They might disapprove of religious mania.

ANNIE. Well, of course, Leonora, I am a very religious type. That is something that very few people understand about me.

CHARLIE. Annie, be careful what you say. I think it highly possible that Leonora's posing as an object of pity simply to see how we react. We've got our eyes on you, Leonora. (*Exit.*)

LEONORA. I think I ought to go away. I've played on Charlie's nerves.

CATHERINE. He would be far more worried if you left.

ANNIE. He would think you weren't going to leave your money to Daphne.

DAPHNE. That's unfair to my father, Annie.

LEONORA. It isn't unflattering to him as a father.

CATHERINE. We would feel terribly guilty if you left just now, Leonora. — As if we'd failed you after all these years.

ANNIE (*goes through French windows*). It's going to be marvellous on the canal this afternoon.

CATHERINE. Daphne, why don't you go out on the boat with Annie? You look moony.

DAPHNE. No, I couldn't possibly. I feel sick. Besides, I've nothing suitable to wear in a boat with Annie. (*Exit.*)

LEONORA *follows* ANNIE *on to terrace.*
Light fades on CATHERINE.
Light up on ANNIE *and* LEONORA *on terrace obliquely facing canal.*

ANNIE. I think you came through that ordeal magnificently.

LEONORA. Yes, I saved a certain amount of face.

ANNIE. It was quite a drama, Leonora.

LEONORA. Saving face is essentially a dramatic instinct for those who insist on playing heroic parts.

ANNIE. But you are a heroine. They were quite unprepared for you. So was I, of course, but then I'm always prepared for things I'm unprepared for. Whatever will you do next?

LEONORA. It will have to be something suitably dramatic, won't it?

ANNIE. Let me see. You mustn't, of course, go near a psychiatrist, unless you were thinking of eloping with him. But they aren't satisfactory. One can't lean on them when it comes to the leaning point. In my experience — well, I say no more, but take it from me they aren't any good. You couldn't elope with Charlie, I suppose?

LEONORA. Charlie hasn't proved responsive to my overtures, Annie.

ANNIE. I quite agree. There is no chivalrous spirit in Charlie. What about eloping with Daphne's boy friend? He doted on you, obviously, at first sight, although of course he said little.

LEONORA. Young Charlie had better stick to Daphne. She's pregnant.

ANNIE. She isn't!

LEONORA. She is.

ANNIE. How thrilling! Who told you?

LEONORA. The symptoms told me.

ANNIE. Do they know?

LEONORA. Not yet.

ANNIE. I never thought young Charlie had it in him. I suppose he is the man?

LEONORA. I think so. The symptoms tell me he is.

ANNIE. Well, you certainly can't elope with him.

LEONORA. I had better disappear.

ANNIE. It wouldn't be dramatic enough. They wouldn't know what had happened to you, and it would all be a worry and a mess.

LEONORA. I have thought of a dramatic way. Imagine Catherine, Charlie and Daphne sitting out here on the terrace after dinner. (*Pointing to chairs.*) Catherine, Charlie, Daphne. It's just gone nine, not quite dark yet. Mrs. S. has gone home. They are discussing what to do about Leonora. Daphne says Leonora must see a psychiatrist. Catherine says yes, but how can we make her see that? Charlie says, the woman is going through the menopause, it's obvious. Catherine says yes, but what do we do about it — Can you envisage the scene, Annie?

ANNIE. Yes, and Daphne keeps saying a psychiatrist.

LEONORA. The girl has to say things like that at a time like this. — Well, while they are all discussing Leonora and her future prospects, a small group of people has gathered down there on the bank of the canal. They have pulled in a body from the water and are attempting to revive it. They are unsuccessful. One of the group recognises the body and points to this house. It is carried up the steps

and laid at the feet of Catherine, Charlie and Daphne,
who are still discussing what to do about Leonora. — It
is then that they stop discussing Leonora and her future.

ANNIE. It's thrilling! It makes me run hot and cold. But
I wouldn't stage that one if I were you, Leonora, because
you wouldn't be able to enjoy it. I mean, what's the use
of having a dramatic sense if you go and get drowned
just before the climax?

LEONORA. I've thought of that.

ANNIE. But it's a brilliant idea to stage your climax out here
on the terrace. It's a perfect setting, and you needn't get
wet if it rains. Stick to bricks and mortar, Leonora, they
are much safer than the canal.

LEONORA. Are they?

ANNIE. Oh, much.

LEONORA. Look. (*Takes hold of a tall pillar. It moves.*) It
doesn't look very safe to me.

ANNIE. Leonora, what are you doing?

LEONORA (*shaking the terrace wall*). It blows all your theories
to hell, doesn't it?

ANNIE. It's thrilling! It gives me a horrible feeling. Do it
again, Leonora.

LEONORA (*shaking pillar*). I blow all your theories to hell and
you tell me it's thrilling.

ANNIE. I think it's a brilliant discovery of yours, Leonora.

LEONORA. Some people have known it all their lives. The
scenery is unreliable, Annie. Some people know that by
instinct, they take it for granted.

        Enter MRS. S.

MRS. S. Annie there? The boat's ready, Charlie says. He'll
give you a shove off.

ANNIE. I'm coming right away.

MRS. S. Daphne's expecting. Craving for cucumbers. Vomiting 6 a.m.

Puts straight a bit of the set which LEONORA *has displaced.*

ANNIE. Do they know?

MRS. S. Certainly not. They are deep thinkers, my dear, not common detectives. Doctors of philosophy, not medicine. Must a happened at Oxford.

Fade and lights up on terrace at dusk. CATHERINE, DAPHNE, CHARLIE, *who sit squarely facing the audience.*

DAPHNE. I don't see why she can't be forced to go to a psychiatrist.

CHARLIE. An audience, she says, eyes upon her. The next thing, she'll be saying we're on the stage.

DAPHNE. I mean, if one needed to consult an ordinary doctor, one would be obliged to consult an ordinary doctor. I don't see why Leonora should get away with it just because her trouble is mental.

CATHERINE. I think a nursing home would be the all-round answer, Daphne.

DAPHNE. What did you say?

CATHERINE. Somewhere peaceful with a private room. Leonora needs a rest.

CHARLIE. There's something going on down on the bank. See the crowd. Someone's fallen in the water. (*Stands up to look.*)

DAPHNE *and* CATHERINE *stand up to look.*

CATHERINE. Go and see who it is, Charlie.

DAPHNE. Oh, I feel sick.

LEONORA *appears from the French windows behind them.*

LEONORA. What's going on down there?

CATHERINE⎫ Oh!

DAPHNE   ⎬ Oh! Leonora. I wish you wouldn't creep up
         ⎭ behind people.

LEONORA. There's been something going on down on the
canal for the past five minutes. I saw it from my window.
I think someone must have fallen in. I'm going down.
(*She runs down the steps towards the canal.*)

CATHERINE. One isn't much use in a crowd, or I'd——

CHARLIE. There's a chap carrying somebody.

CATHERINE. He's coming over here. Look!

CHARLIE *goes down the steps.*

Enter CHARLIE BROWN, *dripping wet, carrying* ANNIE,
dripping wet, followed by LEONORA *and* CHARLIE.

ANNIE. My boat capsized. I was rescued by Charlie Brown.
Isn't he a hero? He just dived in and fished me out.
What a crowd I drew! It's just as well I was suitably
dressed.

CHARLIE BROWN *sets her down.*

CATHERINE. Come and get dry immediately, Annie.

CHARLIE. Come indoors, both of you. I can't afford a
scandal.

ANNIE. The water's extremely wet to night, Leonora.

CURTAIN

END OF ACT TWO

ACT THREE

The same room.

CHARLIE. She'll have to leave home immediately.

CATHERINE. Charlie, how can I think of the practical side of things if you only talk?

CHARLIE. It's my duty to talk. I can't afford to feed another mouth. The house is full of mouths to feed. She'll have to leave immediately.

CATHERINE. The baby will not be born immediately.

CHARLIE. Well, she'll soon be eating for two.

CATHERINE. She's eating cucumber salad almost exclusively.

CHARLIE. I can't afford to provide special diets.

CATHERINE. Take a drink if you can't face the facts.

CHARLIE. I can't afford a drink. I've wasted a fortune on the girl's education and she's gone and spent it on fornication and cucumbers. She'll have to pack her bags and——

CATHERINE. She's got nowhere to go. Shut up, Charlie.

CHARLIE (*pouring himself a drink*). She'll have to go to a home for fallen women. I'm not going to have any infants in this house at my age. Nappies on the line. I've had quite enough of your relations, Catherine, and I don't want any more in the house.

CATHERINE. She's arranging to get married as soon as possible, she says. In fact that's all I could get out of her.

CHARLIE. She can't have a wedding out of my pocket, if that's what she means. If she wants a wedding, let him pay for the wedding.

CATHERINE. You didn't pay for our wedding.

CHARLIE. I wasn't to blame for our wedding. He's got himself to blame for his. Sorry — my salary doesn't run to champagne. They'd better get married quietly. Hush it up. (*Pours himself another drink.*) And I paid for our honeymoon, don't forget that. I was well out of pocket over the honeymoon.

CATHERINE. Could you afford to give me a gin and lime?

CHARLIE. It's a bit early to start. (*Pours gin and lime for* CATHERINE.) Do you mean to tell me she actually wants to marry that fellow?

CATHERINE. Well, she'll have to.

CHARLIE. What do you mean, 'she'll have to'. You can't force an innocent young girl to marry a man not of her own choice just because she was taken in by his clever slick talk. I know that sort of swine, I've seen them at work, my dear woman, believe it or not.

CATHERINE. She could have an operation.

CHARLIE. If she has any illegal operations, out of my house she goes. It might kill her. I can't afford to have police enquiries. Out she goes with her abortions and expensive funerals. If you would only keep calm about this, Catherine, you wouldn't panic. You wouldn't be advocating suicidal solutions like abortions and marriage. After all, she's your daughter.

CATHERINE. I advocate nothing. It's her business. I think she's very fortunate in the circumstances. Very lucky indeed.

Enter MRS. S. *with tray of coffee.*

CHARLIE. Poor Daphne.

CATHERINE. I say poor Charlie, I'm rather sorry for poor young Charlie.

MRS. S. 'Phone message for Daphne. They want the machine back.

CHARLIE. Sorry for him? Sorry for him?

MRS. S. It's gone from the broom cupboard again. Walked.

CATHERINE. It's over there by the window. Yes, I'm sorry for him.

MRS. S. (*picks up tape recorder*). Hope it isn't too heavy for her to carry. (*Moves it up and down.*)

CHARLIE. I've never heard of anything so unnatural. You are sorry for your daughter's seducer.

MRS. S. (*sets tape recorder on table*). Drink your coffee. Fancy starting on the bottle before eleven just because Daphne's failed in her Ph.D. How does it work?

CHARLIE. She may still take her degree.

CATHERINE. Oh no, Charlie. Oh no, Charlie. Mrs. S., I wouldn't play about with it in case it breaks.

CHARLIE. Oh yes, Catherine. Arrangements could be made for her to continue her studies. Mrs. S., if you break it, I can't afford——

MRS. S. *switches on machine.*

LEONORA'S VOICE. Charlie, give me a child, I want a child.

CHARLIE. Turn it off.

CHARLIE'S VOICE. Leonora——

MRS. S. *switches it off.*

MRS. S. You better remove the traces, Charlie, or it might reach the ears of an unseen audience. Shocking. (*Goes out.*)

CHARLIE (*fiddling with machine*). How do you remove the tape?

LEONORA'S VOICE. Charlie, give me a child, I want a child.

      CHARLIE *switches it off.*

CATHERINE. Oh, I can't stand it. Charlie, I want Leonora to leave this house.

CHARLIE. Why?

CATHERINE. We have enough mouths to feed.

LEONORA'S VOICE. Charlie, give me a chi—— (*Switched off.*)

CATHERINE. Charlie, stop it!

CHARLIE. I'm trying to remove the tape. If I hadn't thought of it you would have let it go back to its owner with this incriminating tape inside it.

      Enter ANNIE *dressed 'for lunch at the Ritz'.*

ANNIE. I am lunching at the Ritz, if you must know.

CATHERINE. I haven't asked you where you're going, Annie.

ANNIE. You spoke with your eyes, Catherine. You said 'Where the hell do you think you're going?'

CHARLIE. Who is taking you to lunch?

ANNIE. I am taking young Charlie to lunch.

CHARLIE. Young Charlie has suddenly become the focus of flattering attention in this household. He rapes my daughter and you take him to the Ritz.

LEONORA'S VOICE. . . . child, I want a child.

CATHERINE. Oh stop it, Charlie!

ANNIE. My dear, men are so extremely sentimental about their virile attractions. You must realise it isn't every day that a handsome woman like Leonora makes a suggestion of that type. Naturally, Charlie wants to play it over and over again, it's only natural.

CATHERINE. Leonora is not as handsome as she used to be.

CHARLIE. I want to get this tape out of the machine and burn it, actually.

ANNIE. That's what they do with our love letters, I'm convinced of it. They read them over and over again, then, in despair, they burn them. Once a man starts burning your communications to him, you may be sure he's beside himself.

CATHERINE. Leonora is to leave this house.

ANNIE. That's quite the wrong way to handle the situation, Catherine. In my opinion the wife should always befriend the other woman in the case.

CHARLIE. I have the impression that Leonora would like to leave us but . . . I think she would really like to go, but . . .

ANNIE. But she can't tear herself away from you, Charlie darling.

CATHERINE. Leonora is a witch. She has had an insidious influence on us during the past three weeks. Look what's happened to Daphne.

CHARLIE. Daphne is more than three weeks pregnant.

ANNIE. Yes, Charlie, but Catherine only discovered it yesterday. Be fair. I'm not taking sides, I only say fair's fair. Don't forget my boat unaccountably capsized on the canal yesterday. Catherine is bound to suspect witchcraft. After all, Catherine isn't a rational sober scholar like you, Charlie.

CATHERINE. There is nothing irrational in what I say. One, Leonora was apparently off her head three weeks ago. Two, now she is apparently recovered. Three, I don't believe she could be cured in that time by natural means. Four——

ANNIE. Why are you counting on your fingers?

CHARLIE. She wants to prove that she has a scholarly mind.

CATHERINE. Four, since it is extremely unlikely that she could have recovered from a serious mental lapse within three weeks by natural means one must look for supernatural means. Hence, it is not entirely unreasonable to suppose that Leonora has been dabbling in witchcraft.

CHARLIE. Shut up.

CATHERINE. Women who practised the black arts in the Middle Ages frequently lost their senses for brief periods and made obscene suggestions.

CHARLIE. It wasn't an obscene suggestion. Leonora only wanted to sleep with me, that's all. A perfectly healthy and natural instinct.

CATHERINE. No, Charlie, no. She didn't say that, she said, 'Give me a child, I want a——'

CHARLIE. I really must get the tape out of this machine. Annie, do you know how it works?

CATHERINE. I shall ask Leonora to leave.

CHARLIE. Shut up.

ANNIE. Don't ask me to touch machines when I've just got my nails beautifully lacquered for young Charlie. Everything must be perfect for Charlie's Ritzy lunch. It's his first and it might be the last. Do you want me to sound young Charlie on what he's prepared to accept in fina. settlement?

CHARLIE. Settlement of what?

ANNIE. The marriage.

CHARLIE. Tell him I'll have him in court for paternity.

LEONORA'S VOICE. . . . a child . . .

     ANNIE *goes out.*

F

CHARLIE. Daphne will have to come and fix this. I've made a mess of it. (*Shouts.*) Daphne!

CATHERINE. You said that Leonora was putting on an act.

CHARLIE. I didn't mean it.

CATHERINE. It's a strange admission for a prospective professor of economics to say that he said what he didn't mean.

CHARLIE. I was not on the lecture platform. One is entitled to say what one doesn't mean in one's own home. (*Shouts.*) Daphne!

Enter MRS. S.

MRS. S. She's upstairs with her stomach. Are young Charlie's ma and pa Ph.D.'s?

CATHERINE. No, they're not.

MRS. S. Are they academics of any variety?

CATHERINE. No, they're in cement.

MRS. S. Well, that's one good thing. It'll improve the stock, if you know your eugenics, not to mention ethnology.

Enter DAPHNE.

DAPHNE. What do you think you're doing? You've unwound it wrong.

CHARLIE. Well, do something, don't just——

DAPHNE (*as she rushes out, sick*). Oh, I'm dying.

MRS. S. You should mind how you speak to Daphne in her condition. What time they coming tonight?

CATHERINE. Seven-thirty for eight.

CHARLIE. Who's coming?

CATHERINE. The Westons are coming to dinner.

MRS. S. Chicken Maryland. Cucumber salad. Daphne won't keep it down. She can't keep down the medicine. Hark at her up there. (*Goes out.*)

CHARLIE. Who are the Westons?

CATHERINE. Young Charlie's parents. We are to discuss the young couple's future.

CHARLIE. I can't afford to discuss the young couple's future. I can't afford to discuss my own future. The future doesn't bear thinking of. The whole world is on the verge of starvation if the population increases at its present rate, and you ask me to discuss the future.

CATHERINE. I'm going to leave you, Charlie. I have decided. I'm going to start a new life.

Enter MRS. S.

MRS. S. Annie's laid out her scarlet velvet to wear tonight. She seems to think that it's going to be an occasion.

CATHERINE. The one with the enormous skirt. Annie will have to pack and go. We owe it to Daphne. Annie must leave us this afternoon.

MRS. S. I told her, I said, 'Annie, it isn't a celebration tonight, it's a sober reckoning of the fruits of sin.'

CHARLIE. If you mean to insult my daughter, Mrs. S., you can go. Your cards are stamped up to date.

CATHERINE. Charlie, I suggest you go and stay at your club, or get a flat somewhere. Just leave the house. I can manage without you, but I can't manage without Mrs. S.

MRS. S. No, Mrs. D., what's said can't be unsaid. I take my cards this instant. Lunch is in the oven, help yourselves.

Enter LEONORA.

LEONORA. I feel terrible.

CHARLIE. What's the matter, Leonora?

LEONORA. I'm frightened.

CATHERINE. Have a drink, Leonora. What's the matter?

LEONORA. I've done something with my life for the first time in my life.

MRS. S. Never!

LEONORA. I've accepted a four-year lectureship in America. I sent off a wire early this morning. I might have a confirmation of the appointment by this evening. It frightens me.

MRS. S. Oh go on, Leonora, have a bash at it.

CATHERINE. Four years!

LEONORA. Four years at least.

CATHERINE. What shall I do without you, Leonora? I depend on my visits to Oxford, and your visits here. We've never been parted for four months together, never mind four years.

CHARLIE. Is there a man behind this, Leonora?

LEONORA. What do you mean?

CHARLIE. I thought you were rather thick with that professor of Ionic Studies from Columbia when he was over here last summer. Self-opinionated and overpaid. Not your type at all, Leonora. What university are you going to?

LEONORA. Columbia.

CHARLIE. Oh, Columbia. Yes, I thought as much. I warn you, Leonora, the man's a——

MRS. S. I quote from Hoffenbinder's *Psychology of the Intellectual*, vol. two, page 368 : 'The academic environment frequently produces inconsistencies of attitude in the private life of the intellectual. In fact, it may be generally concluded that the more consistent the train of thought or public attitude in the developed intellect, the less consistency is to be observed in the private attitudes and utterances of the individual full stop.'

CATHERINE. Yes, quite, Mrs. S. Leonora, we've welcomed you into our home. You've come with us on our holidays. We've given you every consideration and assistance that a family could give. Charlie has filled in your tax returns year after year. And now, just when we've been going out of our minds all morning over Daphne, you walk in and you say you're going to America. You don't mean this?

CHARLIE. Can you do anything with this tape machine, Leonora?

LEONORA. I do mean it. (*Looks at tape machine.*) But I'm afraid. That's all I know.

CURTAIN

END OF SCENE I

ACT THREE

SCENE II

Same day.   Same room.
DAPHNE *fixing tape recorder*.   MRS. S. *watching*.

MRS. S. You got it working all right?

DAPHNE. Yes.

MRS. S. You better take it back before it does any more harm. What did you do with the talkative portion?

DAPHNE. I put it in the stove.   Have you got ten bob on you, Mrs. S. ?

MRS. S. Not today I haven't.   What you want it for?

DAPHNE. I want to send this over to Kensington in a taxi.

MRS. S. Why don't you take it yourself on the bus?   Do you good to get out of all this and see some old friends.   You owe me thirty-five and eight already, you know.

DAPHNE. You can have it on Monday.   I don't want to go to Kensington.   I just don't want to see anybody, any old friends, nobody.

MRS. S. Why not?   You aren't showing yet.   Let's have a look.   I should say you would carry it behind when you start to show.

DAPHNE. I might be sick.   I would be sure to be sick.

MRS. S. Send young Charlie.

DAPHNE. He's having lunch at the Ritz with Annie.   She doesn't ask me to lunch at the Ritz, you'll observe.

MRS. S. You'd a fetched it all up. Waste a money. Send young Charlie when he comes back all aglow with his melon frappé followed by sole meunière accompanied with Chablis followed by Armagnac and wrapped in a cloud of contentment over Annie's talk. 'Darling young Charlie, it's going to be so thrilling having another Ph.D. in the family, especially a handsome one for a change.'

Enter ANNIE.

ANNIE. Charlie is heavenly, Daphne. When he does talk, it's thrilling. He asked me to tell you he's got an appointment this afternoon but he'll be along later with his parents. I met Charlie out there just now, he's got a new van. Where's Charlie, is he in?

DAPHNE. Will you lend me ten bob till Monday, Annie?

ANNIE. Of course, if you mean it literally. But if you're being allegorical I'm afraid I haven't got anything till Michaelmas.

MRS. S. No, you don't spend ten bob on taxi-cabs, if Charlie's outside with a van. (*Goes out on the terrace.*) Charlie! — Here, Charlie, we need your services, my good man.

Enter CHARLIE BROWN.

CHARLIE B. I was just about to pay you a call in any case. Coincidence. Where's the doctor?

MRS. S. Leonora's quit practice. She has taken the step of acceptng a job in America, like they all do sooner or later.

CHARLIE B. (*sitting down*). I have something to unburden myself of to the doctor. Developments in my life. Make us a cup of tea.

MRS. S. *goes.*

DAPHNE. Charlie, could you run this machine over to an address in Kensington for me?

CHARLIE B. Tomorrow morning I could, not today I couldn't. My time's not my own. I'm doing urgent delivery work, TV replacement service. People waiting.

DAPHNE. What time could you take it tomorrow?

CHARLIE B. Ten sharp.

DAPHNE. Annie, could you make a telephone call for me? Kensington 9082. Some people I don't want to talk to, the Dolphins. Tell them the tape recorder will be delivered tomorrow at half past ten.

ANNIE. May I tell Mary you're engaged to marry a charming young nuclear physicist without delay?

DAPHNE. No. Whatever you do, don't mention nuclear physicist. It's a disgrace to be engaged to a nuclear physicist. You just say, 'Daphne is sending Eunice's tape recorder tomorrow at about half past ten.' What are you to say?

ANNIE (*holding imaginary telephone*). Hallo — Mary? This is Annie. I'm lovely, thank you, how are you? Listen, Mary, I've got a message for Eunice from Daphne. She's returning the tape recorder tomorrow at half past ten. Charlie will bring it. No, dear, Charlie Brown, you don't know him. No, Mary, no, Daphne can't come to the telephone, she's got stomach trouble, tell Eunice. No, nothing serious, it will just take time.

> *Enter* MRS. S. *with cup of tea for* CHARLIE.

Will she — ? Just a minute, I'll ask her —. Daphne, will you be fit to sit in Trafalgar Square next week?

MRS. S. No, and a good thing too. It gives you piles sitting on the pavement. Besides, she'll be on her honeymoon.
Goes out.

DAPHNE. That's highly questionable.

ANNIE (*into imaginary telephone*). It's highly questionable. I must run now, Mary, I've got to change for dinner.

I know Mary, I know it's only three-fifteen, but this is a dress rehearsal. Yes, I'll ring again. Goodbye.

CHARLIE B. Good for Annie! You should be on the stage.

ANNIE. Charlie, it's very odd that you should say that. It's exactly what my C.O. in the Wrens said when we were having a little argument about the length of my hair. I said, 'I'm not going to have it cut short, that's all. — Not when I'm having all this success I'm not going to cut off my hair; it goes beautifully with my uniform and my tricorn hat, as you can see for yourself.' Well, she just looked at me and she said, 'You should be on the stage.'

DAPHNE. Kensington 9082.

Exit ANNIE.

LEONORA *enters by French windows.*

CHARLIE B. Hallo doctor, I been waiting for you.

LEONORA. Good afternoon, Charlie. Daphne, how are you feeling?

DAPHNE. Both ways. Physically on the retreat. Mentally in the advance guard, preparing for a big offensive.

CHARLIE B. You put that very neat, Miss. Personally, I'm the other way about, physically like a tank regiment but me mind is on the run. I come to see the doctor about it.

LEONORA. You've met a suitable young lady, Charlie?

CHARLIE B. I've met three.

LEONORA. You will have to make up your mind between them.

CHARLIE B. I don't fancy any of them. You know those reading lamps? I didn't buy one. Couldn't make up my mind.

LEONORA. You will have to let things drift.

CHARLIE B. No, I'm one of those people that's fated to do something because——

DAPHNE. So am I, Charlie.

CHARLIE B. You getting married soon, so Mrs. S. has intimated.

DAPHNE. It's questionable.

CHARLIE B. That's how I feel about the widow.

LEONORA. You didn't mention a widow.

CHARLIE B. Four kids. She don't feed them properly. She smokes all day and drinks all evening. Nothing much to look at, she's let herself go. She cooks bad. The house is a proper mess.

LEONORA. Well, she's out of the question, isn't she?

CHARLIE B. No. She's in the question.

DAPHNE. Do you love her, Charlie?

CHARLIE B. Well, that's questionable. But she loves me, that's unquestionable.

LEONORA. That's a very important point, Charlie. You can't afford to overlook that.

CHARLIE B. You're right. I can't overlook it. We've had good times together when we've been together. Four kids, though.

DAPHNE. Do you like children, Charlie?

CHARLIE B. Not so's you'd notice it. I don't mind them. But they like me, they're very fond of me, those kids, I'll say that for them. They look out for me coming. Won't go to bed.

LEONORA. I would consider marrying the widow if I were you, Charlie. It's essential to be loved if you like being loved.

DAPHNE. He might find it a responsibility to be loved without being able to love back. He might be unhappy.

LEONORA. Responsibility is not necessarily an unhappy thing.

DAPHNE. It's better when both are in love.

LEONORA. Both partners are seldom in love to the same degree, or in the same manner. Sometimes, in a person who does not love easily, love arises from necessity.

DAPHNE. I'm damned if I will be pushed into a marriage out of necessity, Leonora.

LEONORA. We're discussing Charlie's case.

DAPHNE. Yes, I know we are discussing Charlie's case. I understand perfectly. There is no necessity in Charlie's case.

LEONORA. It seems to me there must be, or he wouldn't be considering marrying the widow in such a hurry.

CHARLIE B. If I don't marry her she's going to marry someone else. Says she needs a husband. But she likes me best. I got to make up my mind.

DAPHNE. He'd be better with an attractive young girl.

CHARLIE B. They're none of them so loving as the widow is, Miss.

LEONORA. Charlie is attached to the widow. He would regret losing her.

DAPHNE. In their case there is probably no conflict of moral principle. Charlie, if you had to choose between your feelings and your principles in choosing a wife, which would you choose?

CHARLIE B. I would choose the widow.

LEONORA. You're a true philosopher, Charlie.

DAPHNE. I don't see that he's answered my question. Charlie, what are your views about the Bomb?

CHARLIE B. Oh, very bad. Shocking.

DAPHNE. Would you marry a woman who was employed to help in Bomb experiments?

CHARLIE B. I couldn't say about that. I would have to take a look at the lady in question before I could give you an honest answer to that.

DAPHNE. Leonora, would you marry a man engaged in the type of nuclear research that I mean?

LEONORA. I would have to take a look at the man in question before I could give you an honest answer to that. But in your circumstances I would do so. On principle, if nothing else.

DAPHNE. What do you mean, on principle? You know I'm violently against the Bomb, Leonora. I sometimes wonder if you're human. Doesn't anybody ever think of the unborn children?

LEONORA. I'm thinking of the unborn. One might wonder, Daphne, if you're human.

CHARLIE B. Is the chap nice, Miss?

LEONORA. He loves her and she finds him attractive. Your case, Charlie, appears to be more complex. The widow loves you but you don't find her particularly attractive.

CHARLIE B. Well, I wouldn't say that. We've had some good times, doctor. Ta-ta. (*Goes out abruptly.*)

DAPHNE. Something upset him. Was it us?

LEONORA. No, only the fact that he wants to marry the widow and doesn't want to want it.

DAPHNE. What do you know about love and marriage anyway? Have you ever loved a man?

LEONORA. Not really. I've only had foolish feelings. Sometimes I still have them.

DAPHNE. Have you ever been loved?

LEONORA. I am loved, if you really want to know.

DAPHNE. Who by?

LEONORA. Plainly, a very foolish man.

DAPHNE. Would you give up your principles for him? You wouldn't, would you? I know how strongly you feel, for instance, about celibacy in the dedicated scholar. Would you give that up?

LEONORA. I might feel obliged to do so on principle. If one has committed a folly in the dark, Daphne, one sometimes has to redeem it by another folly in broad daylight.

Enter MRS. S.

MRS. S. Overseas telegram for Leonora. That's about the job, I daresay. Go on, open it.

Fade.
Lights up on CATHERINE *alone, exhausted. She flops on sofa, pours tea.*
Enter ANNIE *in red velvet evening dress.*

CATHERINE. You can't wear that tonight. And why are you dressed so early? It's only five.

ANNIE. I thought this would be a suitable dress to be asked to change out of.

CATHERINE. Annie, I love you being here. You make me feel like an intellectual. Pour some tea. I'm tired. Do you think Mrs. Weston will try to talk to me as woman to woman?

ANNIE. I see no alternative basis of approach.

CATHERINE. If she gets on my nerves I shall discuss Assyrian Palaeography with Leonora. Would that be insufferable?

ANNIE. Yes, it would be most suitably insufferable, in my opinion, Catherine, for an academic household.

CATHERINE. I wish Charlie were a professor, it would sound good.

ANNIE. Do you think I might pass for a Ph.D. if I wore something discreet?

CATHERINE. Perhaps you might leave the word 'thrilling' out of your vocabulary. Scholars are never thrilled, at the most they are excited.

ANNIE. Leonora is thrilled. She got a wire confirming her appointment at Columbia.

CATHERINE. I shall miss her terribly. I wish I were not such a neurotic.

ANNIE. Well, as young Charlie said at lunch today, 'An intelligent woman's neurosis is more valuable than a stupid woman's complacency, and more attractive.'

CATHERINE. He didn't!

ANNIE. He did. I wouldn't have believed he could say such a long sentence.

CATHERINE. Who was he referring to?

ANNIE. You. He thinks you're attractive.

CATHERINE. I wouldn't have thought he had it in him.

ANNIE. He's very upset about Daphne. She told him she would think over his proposal of marriage. Of course, that's the right move — in her circumstances, the only move.

CATHERINE. Poor young Charlie. Daphne's my daughter, but I must admit between ourselves, Annie, that if I were a man I would find her a bit dull.

ANNIE. He must have found a brighter side. I was afraid he might be rather tiresome himself, but actually, when one brings him out of his shell, he's almost thrilling and very amusing. I said to him, 'You really are very witty, Charlie, why don't you say things oftener?' He said, 'People who seldom say anything at all frequently gain a reputation for wit.' I said, 'Have you a reputation for wit among your colleagues?' He said, 'I think so.' I said, 'Go on!' He said, 'Yes.' I said, 'Are you ever quoted?' He said, 'No.' I said, 'Are you ever mis-quoted?' He said, 'No, mine is a very budding reputa-tion, I'm afraid.' I said, 'I think you're terrific.' He said, 'What?' I said, 'I think you're absolutely brilliant. I think you've got a great future ahead of you, Charlie. I suppose you think I'm a very silly woman.' He said, 'No. Most intelligent.'

Enter YOUNG CHARLIE *through windows.*

ANNIE. I was just speaking of you, Charlie. (*To* CATHERINE) . . . most intelligent.

YOUNG CHARLIE. Am I most intelligent?

ANNIE. You know you are, Charlie. There is no need for agitation on that account. Sit down and recover, if that's what you're upset about.

CATHERINE. I think she went out. It's Daphne you want, isn't it?

ANNIE. She went out. Can I get you some fresh tea?

YOUNG CHARLIE. She telephoned half an hour ago. She's decided not to marry me. On principle.

ANNIE. You will have to change your occupation that's all.

CATHERINE. He can't be expected to give up his career, Annie.

ANNIE. Daphne would have to give up hers.

CATHERINE. She had not started a career.

ANNIE. Young Charlie is so brilliant, he could do something different from what he's doing.

YOUNG CHARLIE. She doesn't know what I'm doing.

CATHERINE. She has a theory, unfortunately.

ANNIE. Charlie, you must put her mind at rest and blow all her theories to hell.

CATHERINE. That's one of the things she's afraid he is going to do.

ANNIE. We shall work it all out when we see your parents tonight, Charlie. Have you told them that Daphne has refused to marry you?

CHARLIE. No.

ANNIE. Good. Then we can spring it on them, and take the wind out of their sails. That will be our first move. The naturally hostile spirit between in-laws can then be exploited in a friendly atmosphere. It's only right that Daphne should be unobtainable.

YOUNG CHARLIE. That's a nice dress.

CATHERINE. Annie's going to change into something less formal. We want to give the right impression of the family as a whole, and so Annie has kindly agreed to give the wrong impression of herself.

YOUNG CHARLIE. You look nice, Annie.

ANNIE. Charlie, when you do decide to speak, it sounds terrifically eloquent. (*Exit.*)

YOUNG CHARLIE. Annie looks nice.

CATHERINE. Nicer than Daphne?

YOUNG CHARLIE. Daphne's different.

> DAPHNE *appears at the French windows with the tape recorder. She silently places it on a table, switches it on, and withdraws unobserved by* CATHERINE *and* YOUNG CHARLIE.

CATHERINE. Annie is attractive.

YOUNG CHARLIE. I like the red dress.

CATHERINE. You have simple tastes, Charlie. Men whose work has to do with abstractions have simple tastes, don't you think?

YOUNG CHARLIE. I won't discuss my work.

CATHERINE. I don't see that there will be anything at all to discuss if Daphne refuses to marry you.

YOUNG CHARLIE. She will have to marry me for the sake of the child.

CATHERINE. That's a grim view of things, I must say.

YOUNG CHARLIE. It's grim that she doesn't love me enough to marry me. She didn't mind going to bed with a nuclear-physicist.

CATHERINE. Daphne is a very complicated girl for a man who has simple tastes in women.

YOUNG CHARLIE. Complicated women attract men of simple tastes.

CATHERINE. Do they now? Would you say Leonora was an attractive woman? I mean, like Annie?

YOUNG CHARLIE. I don't know. I'll have a look and see.

CATHERINE. We think there's a man in her life. Or at least the opportunity of one. Do you really want to marry my complicated daughter?

YOUNG CHARLIE. Yes.

CATHERINE. Are you feeling very miserable because she has said she won't marry you?

YOUNG CHARLIE. Not at the moment.

CATHERINE. Why not at the moment?

G

YOUNG CHARLIE. Because I like being flirted with by her complicated mother.

CATHERINE. Charlie, you have a very unexpected cast of mind.

YOUNG CHARLIE. It's a simple mind. If you go on talking on this subject, naturally I shall make love to you.

CATHERINE. What subject?

YOUNG CHARLIE. The relative attractions of women.

CATHERINE. I speak in the academic sense.

YOUNG CHARLIE. I don't listen in the academic sense. (*Kisses her passionately.*) Women are women to me, not ideas.

> *Enter* MRS. S. *with cardboard carton, which she dumps on the floor.*

MRS. S. Found this under the kitchen table. (*Going over to look at tape recorder.*) You don't want to waste the tape. (*Switches it off. Returns to the box.*) Now then. If I'm going to stop overnight to help you out with the dinner, you got to listen to me, Mrs. D. (*Picks out hot-water bottle.*) What you want to throw this away for?

CATHERINE. It's finished, it's got a leak. Charlie, I think I'm insulted.

MRS. S. What did you throw it away for, then? You should of chucked it out. This is the box for throwing things away. Objects is of no use to me if they got a leak, what's the use of me taking them home? Be more careful in the future. It should a been chucked out.

CATHERINE. Anyway, I just am not satisfied.

MRS. S. (*bringing out pyjama trousers*). And what you want to throw this away for?

CATHERINE. I forget. There must be some reason. Charlie, I don't know what to do with you.

MRS. S. Ought to be chucked out. Gone at the knee. Have you got the top to it, Mrs. D.?

CATHERINE. No, I chucked it out last week. I must go and get ready.

MRS. S. You don't want to waste the cord. It might do for tying up things that you want to chuck out.

Enter DAPHNE *with telegram.*

DAPHNE. A wire for Father.

CATHERINE. I think I know what it is. I'm dying to open it. I wonder if I ought?

DAPHNE. Your delicacy is unbelievable.

YOUNG CHARLIE. Daphne——

Exit DAPHNE *through window.*

CATHERINE (*opens telegram*). It's Charlie's new appointment. That means he's a Professor of Economics — confirmation to follow. Oh well, I'm glad this has happened before the party. (*Goes out.*)

Fade.
Lights up on empty room after dinner.
Noises from the dining-room.
Enter LEONORA, MRS. WESTON *and* ANNIE. ANNIE *is dressed in black skirt, black stockings, white blouse with floppy black tie and heavy-rimmed glasses.*

MRS. WESTON. I always think it's awfully degrading, this habit of having to leave the men after dinner to get down to their serious talk. It makes one feel like an empty chattel, and they always take such a long time to come.

LEONORA. We're supposed to take a long time to powder our noses, Mrs. Weston.

ANNIE. In any case, Mrs. Weston, we here don't depend on the male element to provide intellectual nourishment. The women of this household always engage in a high level of conversation amongst themselves; very high.

LEONORA. In my experience learned women mostly talk about the dreariest things when they withdraw at dinner-parties. They save all their bright talk till the men appear. There's a positively hostile feeling till the men appear. It shouldn't be so, but it is so.

ANNIE. It may be so, Leonora, but you shouldn't be saying so. My point is, that we're not a frivolous set.

LEONORA. Frivolity isn't the only alternative to dreariness. Let's not give Mrs. Weston the impression that we're a dreary set.

ANNIE. I disagree. On the whole, I think Mrs. Weston should have the impression that we are quite impersonal and as dreary as hell.

MRS. WESTON. My dears, we're all going to be great friends. Herbert and I have made that decision in spite of the circumstances. When we heard the news, Herbert said to me, 'Now look, we've got to like them or lump them, so we'd better like them.' And when Herbert says a thing, believe me, he means it.

ANNIE. What are your husband's other names, Mrs. Weston?

MRS. WESTON. He has no other names. (*Enter* CATHERINE.) Plain Herbert Weston.

ANNIE. We wondered if he might be a Charlie, which would have been confusing. The Professor is a Charlie, and your son is a Charlie, we call him young Charlie.

LEONORA. Which Professor is a Charlie?

CATHERINE. Charlie has had unofficial news, Leonora.

LEONORA. Oh I see. Splendid.

Enter DAPHNE.

MRS. WESTON. And we may have an even younger Charlie before we know where we are ! Perhaps he'll be a scholar like his father.

ANNIE. Daphne is also a scholar. I have high hopes of Daphne, personally, when she is able to continue her studies.

MRS. WESTON. Oh, she won't have much time for studies, believe me.

ANNIE. I speak from an academic point of view, of course, it's ingrained in us, I'm afraid. It runs in the family.

CATHERINE. You're being very practical, Mrs. Weston. The more practical thing, of course, would be for Daphne to employ a well-trained nurse with a suitable domestic staff.

MRS. WESTON. Well that's funny, on Charlie's pay, isn't it, Daphne ?

DAPHNE. It's the funniest thing I've ever heard in my life. I'm not remotely interested in Charlie's pay, it doesn't concern me in the least.

ANNIE. The Professor would be mildly disturbed if he could hear you, Daphne.

MRS. WESTON. I'm wondering how Herbert and Charlie are getting on with the Professor in there. My son never has much to say to his father, because of course his job has done that, it's silenced him. Poor Herbert will be rather out of his depth between the two of them. Herbert isn't the studious type. He only studies me ! I've got my little interest in life, though. Of course, it's not so deep as what you're accustomed to. I study herbs.

ANNIE. Herbs the diminutive of Herbert ?

LEONORA. I think Mrs. Weston means herbology. A very vast subject, Mrs. Weston.

MRS. WESTON. Remind me, Daphne, to give you the recipe for Artemisia Absinthium, commonly known as Saint John's Girdle or Wormwood. An infusion of this herb has been recommended for healthy childbearing since the Middle Ages,

    DAPHNE *runs off to be sick.*

and as Tusser wrote in the sixteenth century, 'It is as a comfort for heart and for brain. And therefore to have it, it is not in vaine.' An early belief taught that it was worn by Saint John, hence Cingulum Sanctus Johannis, and was used as a charm against evil. It is also used to this day in country districts as a disinfectant in cases of the measles.

ANNIE. How very thrilling, or rather, I should say, exciting. Do you make up love potions, Mrs. Weston?

MRS. WESTON. Oh, scholars are not interested in love potions, I'm sure.

ANNIE. One takes an impersonal interest in everything, potions, love and all the other superstitions of the Dark Ages — doesn't one, Leonora? Doesn't one, Catherine?

CATHERINE. I take an immediate interest in Daphne. Everything makes her sick. (*Exit.*)

MRS. WESTON. Daphne's Paying the Price.

LEONORA. If you mean her child then it's cheap at the price. If you mean she's paying for anything else then we don't care to hear it.

MRS. WESTON. Well, I'm afraid I'm a realist. It's inevitable that an unmarried mother should be more inconvenienced than a married mother, as there's more nervous strain.

ANNIE. A realist might say she isn't yet an unmarried mother.

MRS. WESTON. A realist might say she was very fortunate in the circumstances. I'm proud that my son has a sense of honour.

LEONORA. You make it a moral question, Mrs. Weston?

ANNIE. Because that's what we feel you're making it.

MRS. WESTON. Well, of course, morals come into it. I've been a member of the Mothers' Union for twenty-three years, my dears, and I've done a lot of welfare work in that capacity as well as doing my little bit to help Herbert when a case like this crops up in his business. Both Charlie and Daphne are answerable for their morals.

LEONORA. To whom?

MRS. WESTON. To God and Society.

LEONORA. Then they are not answerable to us. We are not God and as there are no men present, we can't propose to represent Society. I think the subject is improper for us.

ANNIE. And we're devoted to Daphne, we won't hear a word against her.

MRS. WESTON. You scholars are not realists, that's my theory.

ANNIE. Show her realism, Leonora. Go on! Blow all her theories to hell.

> LEONORA *reaches out and gives the wall a push. The ceiling rises, while the wall recedes. Everything then settles back into place.*

MRS. WESTON. Oh, what are you doing? What did you do? I thought——

Enter CATHERINE.

CATHERINE. Mrs. Weston, do you think you could concoct a love potion for Daphne? She's being particularly disagreeable.

MRS. WESTON. Where's Herbert? Why don't they come? I feel very odd. I had a most strange illusion just now, as if the house was shaking. Are these houses flimsy?

LEONORA. Realism is very flimsy.

CATHERINE. Leonora, this is hardly the time for abstractions. I'm afraid my cousin Leonora has no sense of the concrete at all. Can I get you some brandy, Mrs. Weston?

MRS. WESTON. A little water, please. I must have taken a turn.

Enter DAPHNE *with tape recorder.*

DAPHNE. Haven't they come in yet?

MRS. WESTON. No, dear, they are discussing your future, I daresay.

DAPHNE. Well, we'll have to make our own entertainment, I daresay. (*Opens tape recorder.*)

CATHERINE. Daphne, it's not . . .?

DAPHNE. No, it's something new. Are you good at recognising voices, Mrs. Weston?

MRS. WESTON. I don't know, dear, why?

DAPHNE. Because I want you to hear a small portion of a recent performance by your lustful, incestuous monster of a nuclear-physicist son, playing opposite my unprincipled mother.

CATHERINE'S VOICE. Would you say Leonora was an attractive woman? I mean — like Annie?

YOUNG CHARLIE'S VOICE. I don't know. I'll have a look and see.

Enter CHARLIE *and* YOUNG CHARLIE.

CATHERINE'S VOICE. We think there's a man in her life. Or at least the opportunity of one. Do you really want to marry my complicated daughter?

CHARLIE. Sorry, but Weston's father was to blame. He's been telling funny . . . What's going on?

YOUNG CHARLIE. Who? What?

YOUNG CHARLIE'S VOICE. Yes.

CHARLIE. Daphne, it's not . . .?

CATHERINE'S VOICE. Are you feeling very miserable because she has said she won't marry you?

YOUNG CHARLIE'S VOICE. Not at the moment.

DAPHNE. Listen to this bit.

CATHERINE'S VOICE. Why not at the moment?

YOUNG CHARLIE'S VOICE. Because I like being flirted with by her complicated mother.

CATHERINE'S VOICE. Charlie, you have a very unexpected cast of mind.

YOUNG CHARLIE'S VOICE. It's a simple mind. If you go on talking on this subject, naturally I shall make love to you.

CATHERINE'S VOICE. What subject?

CATHERINE. Stop it, Daphne!

YOUNG CHARLIE'S VOICE. The relative attractions of women.

DAPHNE *prevents* CATHERINE *from stopping the machine.*

CATHERINE'S VOICE. I speak in the academic sense.

YOUNG CHARLIE'S VOICE. I don't listen in the academic sense. (*Long kissing sound.*) Women are women to me, not ideas.

MRS. S.'S VOICE. Found this under the kitchen table.

DAPHNE *switches it off.*

MRS. WESTON. Was that part of a play?

DAPHNE. It's what you'd call a realistic part.

YOUNG CHARLIE. Daphne, be sensible.

DAPHNE. Get out of my life, Charlie. Disappear out of my life.

Exit YOUNG CHARLIE *through French windows.*

CHARLIE. Catherine, I must say . . .

MRS. WESTON. I can't stand any more of this, it's . . . Herbert, where is he?

LEONORA. Daphne, I know that you're in difficulties, but I think you're most unpleasant. (*Slaps her face:* DAPHNE *slaps* LEONORA.)

CHARLIE (*calls upstairs*). Weston, I say Weston!

MRS. WESTON (*slapping* DAPHNE). Don't you strike an older woman.

| CATHERINE (*slapping* MRS. W.). Take your hands off my daughter. | ANNIE. Go on, Catherine. That's right, Leonora, just give as good as you get. |

MRS. WESTON (*slapping* CATHERINE). You and your daughter have seduced an innocent young man. Do you . . .?

CHARLIE (*as* LEONORA *moves to slap* MRS. WESTON). Leonora! Remember your invisible audience. Eyes upon you. (LEONORA *hesitates then proceeds to slap* MRS. WESTON *regardless.*)

Fade.
Lights up later in the evening. CHARLIE, ANNIE *and* LEONORA *sit drinking in dejected silence for some moments.*

CHARLIE. Where's Catherine?

LEONORA. Out on the terrace looking at the stars.

CHARLIE. She's been looking at the stars for the last half hour.

LEONORA. Twenty minutes.

CHARLIE. This is no time to be looking at the stars for twenty minutes. (*Calls*.) Catherine!

CATHERINE (*from terrace*). Coming in a minute.

LEONORA. We've been looking at each other for twenty minutes.

ANNIE. I haven't been looking at each other for twenty minutes. I've been looking at the problem from various angles. I see everyone's point of view, which is very confusing. Seeing everyone's point of view is like mixing your drinks.

CHARLIE. You've been mixing your drinks, all right.

ANNIE. It's terrible to feel that one's host is watching every sip and every mouthful. I wish someone would send me a bunch of flowers to restore my confidence. Why do they never come at the moment I need them?

CHARLIE. The place is cluttered up with your flowers. (*Calls*.) Catherine! — Why does she go and look at the stars when we're busy discussing a family crisis? (*Calls*.) Catherine!

ANNIE (*turning in her chair to look out*). Shout at her politely, Charlie, she's talking to someone.

CHARLIE. Why is she talking to someone at this time of night? She's always wasting her time gossiping with the neighbours. A higher education was wasted on Catherine. Like mother like daughter.

Enter CATHERINE *from terrace*.

CATHERINE. Haven't you gone to bed yet?

CHARLIE. Well, what an utterly stupid question. Like mother like daughter. Only fit for married life.

ANNIE. Daphne isn't fit for married life if you mean she's got to marry into that family.

CHARLIE. She won't have the chance now.

ANNIE. Most unsuitable. I shall adopt the baby, and Daphne can either continue her studies or marry the man of her choice.

LEONORA. I shall adopt the baby.

ANNIE. I spoke for it first.

LEONORA. No, if you recall, I spoke for it first.

ANNIE. You spoke to the wrong Charlie. I shall speak to the right Charlie.

CATHERINE. You're neither of you fit to adopt any baby. We shall speak to Daphne, and we shall adopt the baby. If all else fails.

CHARLIE. All else has failed, but we can't afford to adopt the baby. I'll have to resign.

CATHERINE. Why?

CHARLIE. Well, when word gets round that my wife is a seducer of young graduates . . .

CATHERINE. Young Charlie attempted to seduce me. Where's that tape? — I can prove it. Not that I hold it against him. Where . . .

ANNIE. Daphne took it up with her. But if I were you, Catherine, I should try to preserve that record for always. It's most flattering, when you come to think of it.

CATHERINE. Do you think so, Annie?

ANNIE. Well, to be quite frank, I'm afraid he didn't attempt to kiss me, although he had every opportunity to do so.

CHARLIE. Any normal woman would regard it as an insult. Any normal woman would have slapped his face.

CATHERINE. I'm not a normal woman, thank you very much.

CHARLIE. It's a question of your dignity. Leonora would have slapped his face. Any woman of normal instincts——

LEONORA. I'm not a normal woman, Charlie, thank you very much.

ANNIE. You must not insult us like this, Charlie. We aren't the sort of women who go round assaulting affectionate young men.

CHARLIE. I see. You only assault each other.

LEONORA. The circumstances were exceptional. Mrs. Weston would bring out the slapping instinct in anyone. I must say, I rather enjoyed it.

CATHERINE. Me too.

Enter MRS. S. *to clear up the litter.*

MRS. S. This is the last time I stop overnight to help you out. If I want a free-for-all I can get it at my sister's place. (*Pours herself a whisky.*) They like to bring the evening to a boil. It isn't any holiday for me to stop here overnight and be witness to a free-for-all. Mrs. D., are you aware of a large bunch of flowers on the floor of the downstairs lavatory?

CATHERINE. Oh! The flowers . . . I forgot all about them. I'll go and get them, Annie, they're lovely.

ANNIE. What a brilliant oversight! (CATHERINE *goes out.*) You see, Charlie, what rational people like you and Leonora don't realise, is that there's a mysterious force that provides for the needs of simple-minded ordinary women like me.

MRS. S. They've been laying in the lav without water for six hours. Won't last. (*Pours herself a whisky.*) I don't know about you lot, but I'm going to bed.

CHARLIE. We're all going to bed.

Enter CATHERINE *with flowers.*

ANNIE. Roses at midnight, how thrilling! Who can they be from? (*Looks at envelope attached.*) They've been sent by Transatlantic Cable . . . America, now who . . .? (*Looks closely at envelope.*) Oh, it's addressed to Leonora. I say, Leonora, how thrilling, someone in America's sent you some roses. Open them up at once.

LEONORA *opens envelope and reads message.*

CHARLIE. There isn't any more room for any more flowers in the house. We've got nothing but flowers all over the place, using up oxygen.

CATHERINE. What a lovely surprise!

ANNIE. Leonora doesn't look very surprised.

LEONORA. Really, do you think I've never had flowers before?

CHARLIE. Arriving in the middle of the night, that's the significant point. (*Looks at envelope.*) By Cable. Expensive shop, must have cost a fortune, it would have kept an Indian peasant for a year.

DAPHNE *rushes in.*

DAPHNE. I've just found a note from Charlie. It was lying on the door-mat. But I can't read it, it's in Greek, signed Charlie in English. Leonora . . . Mother . . . read it.

CATHERINE. Let me see.

LEONORA *looks over* CATHERINE'S *shoulder at the note.*

MRS. S. Sounds like he's done away with himself. Too cryptic for my liking.

LEONORA. It's a quotation from the Greek Anthology.

CATHERINE. So it is. It's a well-known epitaph.

CHARLIE. Let's hear it.

DAPHNE. Translate.

LEONORA. 'Stranger, tell the Lacedaemonians that we lie here, obedient to their commands.'

MRS. S. A very moving farewell, that one is.

DAPHNE. I didn't know he knew any Greek.

CHARLIE. Suicides never announce their departure. They just go and do it.

LEONORA. I have heard of suicide notes being left.

MRS. S. My brother-in-law left a parting note before he turned on the gas. I'd like to tell you what he wrote — but no, it's too macabre. I just couldn't.

CATHERINE. I think this is a hoax.

MRS. S. You should a seen my brother-in-law's farewell — but no, I couldn't repeat it. Sorry, I just couldn't. Talk about nostalgie de la boue !

CHARLIE. Does young Charlie possess a gun or anything ?

DAPHNE. Oh no. He doesn't believe in shooting anything whatsoever.

CHARLIE. No, I suppose that would be unnecessary in his job.

ANNIE. Can young Charlie swim ?

DAPHNE. Yes, but he wouldn't if he was trying to drown himself, now would he ?

MRS. S. If they don't know how to go about it, they struggle for life and save themselves at the last minute. But the really experienced suicide cases always attach a weight to themselves and jump in with their boots on.

ANNIE. Don't you think we should ring the police ?

CATHERINE. That's too drastic. We don't want our name in the papers just now. Charlie's appointment still has to be confirmed.

DAPHNE. I think you're a monster.

LEONORA. Perhaps, after all, it's a hoax.

DAPHNE. Don't listen to her, Leonora — she hasn't a scrap of natural affection. She ought to see a psychiatrist. I'm going to ring the police. They must drag the canal.

CATHERINE. Very well. I shall ring the police (*Goes out followed by* ANNIE).

DAPHNE. How did the victims in the epitaph die, Leonora?

LEONORA. On the field of battle in Thermopylae.

CHARLIE. He evidently sees himself in a very heroic light. Sheer conceit.

MRS. S. You should have heard my brother-in-law's case. Far more stirring than this. But you couldn't a heard it. The court was cleared at the inquest for the reading of the note. And you couldn't a read it. *News of the World* wouldn't touch it. Too hot. (*Lifts* YOUNG CHARLIE's *note and holds it up to the light, looking at it for a few seconds.*) Queen's Velvet.

DAPHNE. I told him to disappear out of my life. But I didn't say out of his.

Enter CATHERINE.

Are the police coming?

CATHERINE. No. I funked it.

DAPHNE. I'm going——

MRS. S. Hark! There's something going on. (*Goes out on terrace followed by the others.*) Here we are. Stand back. (*Pushes them all back.*) They've got the body.

CHARLIE (*going out to terrace*). What's going on?

DAPHNE. The body! Let me see.

LEONORA. Daphne, sit down and keep quiet.

Enter CHARLIE BROWN, *carrying the limp body of* YOUNG CHARLIE. *Both are dripping wet.*

CHARLIE B. I just got him when he was going down the fourth time.

CHARLIE. Someone go and ring the doctor.

CATHERINE. It's unnecessary to ring the doctor. He's still breathing.

CHARLIE. My wife's gone mad. Of course we must have a doctor. Leonora — the number's on the thing. — The National Health doctor, of course.

LEONORA *goes out.*

We'll have to work on him, I suppose.

DAPHNE. I know what to do. Stand back, everybody.

CHARLIE B. I don't know that he hasn't gone, Miss.

DAPHNE *administers first aid to* YOUNG CHARLIE, *pumping and breathing.*

MRS. S. She'll lose it, if she goes on like that. (*Exit.*)

CATHERINE. Let me take a hand, Daphne, I know what to do.

DAPHNE. You're not going to touch him.

CHARLIE B. He's opening his eyes. Not before time.

LEONORA *returns, with towels.*

CHARLIE. The doctor coming?

LEONORA. No, I funked it. Doctors get aggrieved at night, unless there's an emergency.

CATHERINE. You are quite right, Leonora.

CHARLIE. This is an emergency. Get off that man at once, Daphne.

LEONORA (*to* CHARLIE BROWN) I'd go and get dry in the kitchen if I were you, Charlie.

CHARLIE B. You're not in my shoes now, Doctor. This is real-life drama. I want to see the outcome.

DAPHNE. He's closed his eyes again.

Enter MRS. S. *with hot drinks.*

MRS. S. Guess what Annie's doing.

CATHERINE. Changing into something suitable.

DAPHNE. Charlie, are you all right?

YOUNG CHARLIE. Carry on, it's lovely.

CHARLIE. Daphne, stop kissing him in that obscene way in the full electric light. Sit up, Charlie. Daphne, remember this man is an attempted suicide, and suicide is a mortal sin. I'd better get him upstairs and out of his things.

DAPHNE. Are you all right, Charlie?

YOUNG CHARLIE. Oh yes, I mean horribly wet. . . . Cheers. (*Walks out.*)

DAPHNE (*to* CHARLIE BROWN). Don't forget to take my tape recorder to Kensington tomorrow, Charlie, whatever you do.

CHARLIE. Don't forget to remove the tape, Catherine, whatever you do. (*Goes out with* DAPHNE.)

Enter ANNIE.

ANNIE. Has the press arrived? Have the police been? Has the doctor come?

CATHERINE. No, there was no need to dress up.

ANNIE. I was thinking entirely of young Charlie's interests. I would have been arrested instead of him, I would have been photographed instead of him.

CATHERINE. You did that marvellously, Charlie.

CHARLIE B. I thought the young fellow did a good turn. Looked real drowned.

ANNIE. Catherine, you're brilliant! Charlie, you're a hero and a marvellous actor. I saw through the whole thing immediately.

CATHERINE. Well I thought it was time I did something dramatic for a change. Charlie, go and get dry.

MRS. S. I can lend you an old coat that's been chucked out. As soon as I saw that bit of Queen's Velvet I knew it was a frame-up. Young Charlie always puts his private and personal communications to Daphne on Basildon Bond, as I know for a fact. Where would he a got Queen's Velvet at this time of night? He got it off you, Mrs. D. Come on, Charlie.

Exit with CHARLIE BROWN.

LEONORA. Catherine, it was a splendid arrangement.

ANNIE. Did you see through it too, Leonora? Never mind, Catherine, you've made a brilliant start. When you've had more experience of staging things, nobody will see through anything.

LEONORA (*looking at the note*). You've got the accents of the Greek all wrong.

CATHERINE. It was supposed to be young Charlie's Greek, Leonora. I believe in dramatic realism.

LEONORA. English would have been more realistic as he hasn't got any Greek.

CATHERINE. But less dramatic.

Enter CHARLIE BROWN *dressed in an old coat followed by* MRS. S.

Put down some whisky, Charlie.

CHARLIE B. Ta. Congratulations, everyone.

LEONORA. We'll drive you home, Charlie.

CHARLIE B. Got the van outside. I'll be home in two minutes, just round the corner. Better not keep my friend waiting. I got engaged to my friend today.

CATHERINE. Congratulations, Charlie.

LEONORA. Who is it, Charlie?

CHARLIE B. The widow, she wanted me, so I thought she might as well have it her own way.

ANNIE. I always say, Charlie, it's a woman's world when all is said and done. (*Raising glass.*) To Charlie.

CHARLIE B. Thanks. Ta-ta. Nice roses. (*Exit.*)

CATHERINE ⎫
⎬ (*raising glasses*).   Charlie.
LEONORA ⎭

MRS. S. I must sit down to this. (*Sits down and raises glass.*) Charlie.

THE CURTAIN FALLS

THE END